THE TRANSCENDENTAL SAUNTERER

THE TRANSCENDENTAL SAUNTERER

THOREAU AND THE SEARCH FOR SELF

DAVID C. SMITH

FREDERIC C. BEIL
SAVANNAH

gift

818   24.95

12/05

Copyright © 1997 by David C. Smith

First published in the United States by
Frederic C. Beil, Publisher, Inc.
609 Whitaker Street
Savannah, Georgia 31401
http://www.beil.com

First edition

Library of Congress Cataloging-in-Publication Data
Smith, David C. (David Clyde), 1949–
The transcendental saunterer:
Thoreau and the search for self/
by David C. Smith
       p.   cm.
Includes bibliographical references.
ISBN 0–913720–74–7 (alk. paper)
1. Thoreau, Henry David, 1817–1862—
Criticism and interpretation.
2. Transcendentalism (New England).
3. Walking in literature.
4. Self in literature.
I. Title.
PS3054.s63   1992   91–14635
818'.309—dc20   CIP

This book was typeset by Yankee Typesetters, Inc.,
Concord, New Hampshire; printed on acid-free paper;
and sewn in signatures.

CONTENTS

PREFACE

From the moment the first explorer reached the shores of America, walking has been fundamental to the American experience. Throughout their history Americans have celebrated and recorded their walking exploits. Perhaps no American, however, has more comprehensively defined the act of walking than has Henry Thoreau, a nineteenth-century author and transcendentalist. Few individuals have walked as much as Thoreau did; and even fewer have, like Thoreau, applied a holistic approach to walking. Thoreau's *Journal* and his other writings abound with observations about walking. These insights, if we are open to them, can teach us much about living the life of a walker—independent and free-spirited—even in the midst of an oppressive environment. Thoreau's walking experience offers a study in the transcendence of limits, the harmonization with the natural world, the achievement of spiritual growth, and the realization of self-fulfillment. Walking, as Sherman Paul notes, was Thoreau's "most typical mode of action of participation," and it provided him with the "fundamental metaphor of his art of life, his mode of discovery." Walking in nature made possible the heart of Thoreau's transcendental experiences, and his numerous perambulatory forays provided him with a significant expertise about pedestrianism. According to John Christie, "No traveler ever considered himself a better authority on foot travel than Thoreau."

In spite of the apparent importance of Thoreau's walking experience, little attention has been devoted to it. Thoreau remains one of the most celebrated of American nature writers, and his masterpiece, *Walden*, and his other nature essays have deservedly earned considerable popular and scholarly attention. But no one has comprehensively studied the significance of Thoreau's walking experience in nature. Walking was the most important and most consistent physical activity that Thoreau engaged in, yet little is known about his "sauntering," as he liked to call it.

It seems clear that if one is to really understand Thoreau's life and ideas, one must study his walks. Thoreau's walking experience is like a key that opens the door to a fuller understanding of his beliefs and actions. Thus this study examines various aspects of Thoreau's walking experience to determine the impact of sauntering on his life and his writings. This study clarifies the relationship between Thoreau's views on and experiences with perambulating and his own unique brand of transcendentalism, and it establishes the paramount importance to Thoreau studies of a proper understanding of his walking theories and adventures.

This book presents a systematic analysis of Thoreau's sauntering experience, beginning with an examination of the frequency and scope of Thoreau's walks and the compatibility between the act of walking, his transcendental beliefs, and his own unique personality. An analysis of two levels of Thoreau's walks follows, first probing the most basic level of his saunterings—his exploration of nature's surface features—and then studying the deeper level of his internal sauntering and the relationship between walking and the sensory responses, emotions, thoughts, and spiritual insights that were the products of his internal sauntering. Finally, how walking fulfilled Thoreau's essential self is examined, dealing first with the ways that walking helped Thoreau bridge the worlds of nature and society while meeting his conflicting needs for solitude and companionship, and then touching on the ways that walking satisfied Thoreau's need for a vocation and how it aided his efforts to express a personal mythology in his writings.

Quotations from Thoreau's writings are often cited at length. Since there is no collection of his views on sauntering, one purpose of this study is to make available major statements that he made about walking. The new standard edition of Thoreau's writings is the Princeton edition (1971–), replacing the 1906 Walden edition; but since only two *Journal* volumes had been published at the time of this writing, most of the *Journal* citations for this text are taken from the 1962 two-volume reprint of the 1906 edition. Except when another source is attributed, all Thoreau quotes in the text are taken from this edition of the *Journal*. Wherever a Princeton *Journal* volume is cited in the text, the word "Princeton" appears in the in-text reference. Unless indicated otherwise, references to Thoreau's essays and to *Cape Cod* are taken from *The Writings of Henry David Thoreau* (Walden edition, 1906). Emerson's essays are cited from *The Complete Works* (Centenary edition, 1979).

ACKNOWLEDGMENTS

I wish to express my thanks to the following individuals:

—William Shurr, whose timely responses and warm, affirming manner made my tasks all the more rewarding, and whose personal standard of scholarship has instilled in me a desire to excel in my professional life;

—Allison Ensor, whose very helpful manner rescued me from difficulties several times, and whose careful reading of this study helped make possible a quality final draft;

—George Hutchinson, whose trenchant insights into aspects of Thoreau's sauntering experience challenge me to continue my study of this topic, to explore more deeply issues that presently lie only on the surface;

—Cathy Matson, whose willingness to lend help at very busy times and whose probings into the historical context of Thoreau's saunterings have been much appreciated;

—Merlene Ogden, whose personal enthusiasm for Thoreau studies and whose classes on Thoreau and transcendentalism first sparked my interest in what is now a passion and a joy; and

—Deric and Mary Ann Beil, whose friendship has enriched my life and whose hours of editorial labors have resulted in a more readable text.

INTRODUCTION

On a harsh January day in 1857 a solitary figure made his way through the nearly deserted streets of Concord and disappeared from sight as he took the road leaving town. Behind him, Concordians basked in the warmth of their homes and businesses, their voices and activity driving the stillness from the village. Where the man walked, only the sounds of the wind and creaking branches disturbed the quiet of a winter's afternoon.

Careful to avoid being seen by the country dwellers whose houses he passed, the walker charted his own path, crossing fields, fording creeks, foraging through thickets, trudging through swamps, and sauntering into the heart of the forest. Relentlessly he pursued complete solitude and oneness with nature.

Traversing snow-powdered ground, the rambler Henry Thoreau paused to jot notes onto paper—notes that record the spiritual essence of his sauntering experience: "There is nothing so sanative, so poetic, as a walk in the woods and fields even now, when I meet none abroad for pleasure. Nothing so inspires and excites such serene and profitable thought. . . . I come to my solitary woodland walk as the homesick go home. I thus dispose of the superfluous and see things as they are, grand and beautiful. . . . I am aware that most of my neighbors would think it a hardship to be compelled to linger here one hour, especially this bleak day, and yet I receive this

1

sweet and ineffable compensation for it. It is the most agreeable thing I do."

When Thoreau returned to Concord late in the day, his rejuvenated spiritual and intellectual energy contrasted sharply with what he considered the appalling ordinariness and spiritual dearth of the lives of the villagers. Content with their conventional existence, few of his townsmen understood the nature of Thoreau's walking experience. The villagers who saw him—a gaunt shadow against the winter twilight—as he trudged down the streets toward home, shook their heads. Why did he always go walking, especially on miserable days like this? they wondered.

Henry Thoreau, a fierce individualist, cared little for the opinions of his contemporaries. But he cared a great deal about his walks. He once boasted in a letter to a friend, "Even now I am probably the greatest walker in Concord." His claim, made at a time when he was ill, was not inappropriate. Subsequent history has established Thoreau as not only the greatest walker produced in the city of his birth, but also the most notable ambulator of all major American literary figures.

Although many of his contemporaries misunderstood his walking experience, Thoreau's sauntering connects directly with mainstream American experience. The United States has always been a nation of walkers who, like Thoreau, have made walking a central act. Walking has marked the intense pain and bitter disappointment of some of our national failures, the Trail of Tears and the Bataan death march offering two important examples. Walking, such as the first walk on the moon, has helped us celebrate the optimistic fervor and triumphant spirit of our national achievements. And walking has channeled the creative bent of Americans as evidenced in such cultural phenomena as the Mohammad Ali shuffle or Michael Jackson's "moon walk."

American history is full of walkers like Thoreau who had an impact on the national scene. Walking exploits fill the early pages of American history; and during the formative stages of national development, a number of great walkers practiced their art, including George Washington, Daniel Boone, Thomas Jefferson, Benjamin Franklin, and William Cullen Bryant.

Western explorers and mountain men contributed to a significant American walking mythology that emerged in the late nineteenth century. Lewis and Clark, who traveled roughly 5,000 miles for a period of two years, walked most of the way and towed a fifty-five-foot keelboat much of the way up the Missouri River—an astounding accomplishment. Mountain men like John Colter, who outran Indians for six miles, and Hugh Glass, who crawled and walked one hundred miles to a fort after he had been badly mauled by a grizzly bear and left for dead by his companions, contributed not only to the tall tales so typical of American folklore, but also to the importance of walking in the national mythology.

Closely allied with Thoreau, the naturalists made their contribution to the American experience by roaming the American landscape and studying its many features. Walkers like John Muir, William Bartram, John James Audubon, and John Burroughs did much to establish an appreciation for America's natural resources and the importance of its wilderness.

While naturalists traversed the American countryside, other walkers traveled from town to town seeking commercial opportunities. Hikers frequented the roads of the United States before the twentieth century. Peddlers, artists, traveling preachers, vendors, performers, and an assortment of other pedestrians followed the call of the road much as many young men harkened to the call of the sea. One such wanderer, Bronson Alcott, a friend of Thoreau, peddled wares from house to house. Rather than attend Yale, Alcott preferred walking the open road. He could often be seen strutting through Concord in the fancy clothes that he purchased from the profits of his peddling. Alcott's experience was little different from that of many Americans who found adventure in peddling and who were pioneers of our domestic commerce.

In Thoreau's own time, walking became a fashionable form of exercise, commonly practiced at special resorts and places in the country where aristocrats could escape the pressures of city life and rejuvenate their health. Walking has continued since Thoreau's day as a popular form of exercise. Two noted presidents, Kennedy and Lincoln, espoused and exemplified the virtues of the walking experience; and in President Kennedy's time, walking was an especially popular form of exercise. Today nearly two-thirds of all Americans who exercise choose walking over other forms of exercise.

Even the wartime experiences of the United States have reinforced the importance of walking. Gasoline rationing during World War II forced many Americans to walk, resulting in numerous magazine and newspaper articles about the benefits of walking and the formation of walking clubs. Americans not only marched to war, they also marched, as did their forefathers, into the wonders of nature. Such nature walks prepared the way for what Joseph Wood Krutch claimed in 1964 was a rediscovery of nature by the American people. Krutch "saw a return to walking as part of a cultural revolution." He celebrated the Thoreau-influenced return to walking in nature so prominent in the 1960's by proclaiming, "Hurrah for what our fathers used to call shank's mare. Nowadays, 'the man who has everything' is using his legs."

In somewhat typical Thoreau fashion, walking has also been employed by Americans to make political points. In 1954 Supreme Court Justice William O. Douglas, a dedicated walker, defeated a proposal to construct a scenic parkway along the Chesapeake and Ohio Canal by inviting those behind the proposal to walk with him along the entire route of the historical canal—all 180 miles of it. Few were able to complete the entire walk and keep up with Justice Douglas, but his walking effort was sufficient to make his point and preserve the canal tract from the encroachment of the planned parkway. Walking as a political statement was used just as effectively by Martin Luther King and those who participated in the peace marches of the civil rights movement. Other protest marches, such as those dealing with the Vietnam War, abortion, and women's liberation, have also contributed significantly to the American experience.

Long since the time of Thoreau, walking still grips our imagination, as evidenced by the long-term best-seller status of Peter Jenkins' books: *A Walk Across America* (1979) and *The Walk West: A Walk Across America, and Across China* (1981). Americans will continue to walk.

Each American walker has made, and will continue to make, a contribution to American life and culture; but as influential and interesting as these collective walking experiences seem, Thoreau's saunters offer the best insights into the role that walking can play in nurturing the self and fostering spiritual development. His walks offer a testament to the triumph of spirit over flesh, to the transcendence of mind over matter; they reveal much about how the transcendental life can be lived. His rambles celebrate the individualism and idealism that have characterized not only many walkers but Americans in general.

Walking was such an integral part of Thoreau's experience that one cannot understand him without studying his saunters. Alcott once observed: "If one would find the wealth of wit there is in this plain man, the information, the sagacity, the poetry, the piety, let him take a walk with him, say of a winter's afternoon, to the Blue Water,

5

or anywhere about the outskirts of his village-residence" ("The Forester"). Thoreau's walks, when properly understood, reveal much about his personality and beliefs. His walking stride, strategies, partners, experiences, observations, and even his clothing and equipment disclose the unique individual that he was.

Telling us much about Thoreau himself, his walks more importantly speak to man's relationship with his environment. Sauntering Thoreau-style involves the coordinated effort of man's body, soul, and mind in uniting him with the cosmos he inhabits; his spirit enjoys an occult relationship with the universe. Thoreau's walks also reveal much about man's interaction with himself and with others. Involving the human need for solitude, companionship, creative expression, identity, self-integration, and personal fulfillment, Thoreau's rambles help define what man is and what he is capable of achieving.

It is still possible to follow Alcott's advice and take a walk with Henry Thoreau. His walks so permeate his writings that anyone who reads them can vicariously enjoy his saunters with him. This book is an effort to do just this, to attempt to understand Henry Thoreau—his life, his beliefs, and his insights into human nature and man's relationship with the universe—through a study of his walking experiences. It is also a celebration of the walking life—a life which, as Thoreau discovered, frees the self and links it with the divine.

1

THE SAUNTERING LIFE

"I have met but one or two persons in the course of my life who understand the art of Walking, that is, of taking walks," Thoreau observed in his essay "Walking." For Thoreau, walking was a way of life. It involved a spiritual commitment to forsake all and follow the call of the footpath, a point he hyperbolizes in "Walking": "If you are ready to leave father and mother, and brother and sister, and wife and child and friends, and never see them again,—if you have paid your debts, and made your will, and settled all your affairs, and are a free man, then you are ready for a walk."

Walking fulfilled Thoreau's intense desire to know life fully and to live it meaningfully. His walks were serious business. In his *Journal* he admonished, "Resolve to . . . take no walk . . . but such as you can endure to give an account of yourself. Live thus deliberately for the most part." Today we view walking primarily as a form of exercise, but Thoreau in "Walking" advocated a much higher conception of it: "But the walking of which I speak has nothing in it akin to taking exercise, as it is called, as the sick take medicine at stated hours,—as the swinging of dumbbells or chairs; but is itself the enterprise and adventure of the day."

Thoreau described walkers as a "select class" who acquire "a direct dispensation from Heaven to become a walker," and he asserts that one "must be born into the family of walkers." Few could practice as well as Thoreau could the "noble art" of walking and make possible the "requisite leisure, freedom, and independence which are the capital in this profession."

His conception of walking reflects the striking openness to experience that characterized his daily life. This is why the word "saunter" appealed to him. Noting in "Walking" that "sauntering" derived from beggars who roamed the countryside in the Middle Ages and claimed that they were going to the Holy Land, Thoreau pursued its other derivation: *sans terre*. This term, suggesting "without land or a home, which therefore, in the good sense, will mean, having no particular home, but equally at home everywhere," spells "the secret of successful sauntering." To saunter is to meander through life much like a river "sedulously seeking the shortest course to the sea."

Thoreau embraced life with a degree of self-assurance and spiritual fervor seldom experienced by his contemporaries. Sauntering was the method by which he accomplished this. In *sans terre* fashion, he daily rambled into nature, equally at home with the cosmos and with himself. As his legs carried him into the Concord countryside, his spirit flowed with him, following the paths that he charted for himself. His walking life defines the true meaning of sauntering; it reveals the spiritual fulfillment and self-awareness open to one willing to commit totally to the art of walking.

Thoreau's dedication to the sauntering life is evident in the frequency and scope of his walks. He spent more time walking than he did doing any other thing, except sleeping. Walking was, without question, the dominant activity of his life. Alcott labeled Thoreau "a peripatetic philosopher" and noted that he was "out of doors for the best parts of his days and nights" ("The Forester"). E. W. Emerson points out that "for years, a wanderer in the outskirts of our village was like to meet this sturdy figure striding silently through tangled wood or wild meadow at any hour of day or night."

Just how often and how much Thoreau walked can be judged, in part, by his own account in "Walking": "I think that I cannot preserve my health and spirits, unless I spend four hours a day at least—and it is commonly more than that—sauntering through the woods and over the hills and fields, absolutely free from all worldly engagement." Walking four or more hours a day for most of his adult life, Thoreau traversed many miles in the Concord vicinity. William Channing, Thoreau's main walking companion, observed that Thoreau generally, like Walt Whitman, reserved his afternoons for walking, setting out in the early afternoon and returning by supper time. The afternoon walking time was Thoreau's "sacred time."

Thoreau allowed few things to interfere with his walks. One rare exception was the time when he declined a walk in order to help a fugitive slave. Except for scarce instances like this one, Thoreau walked daily, and it was not uncommon for him to saunter after dark. During full moons he frequently walked all night. Even when Thoreau was heavily involved in surveying and commercially growing cranberries, he maintained his walks. Nothing, not even severe Massachusetts winters, could impede Thoreau's sauntering experience, as his February 7, 1855, letter to a friend makes clear: "I still take my daily walk . . . and on the whole have more to do with nature than with man."

The extent of Thoreau's saunterings is as impressive as their frequency. Although most of his walks occurred in the Concord vicinity, he did engage in several lengthy expeditions away from his hometown. These excursions added countless miles to Thoreau's walking mileage and enriched his walking experience, the heart of which belonged to his Concord walks. Thoreau's travels extended to Maine, Canada, Cape Cod, New York, Long Island, the Hudson River Valley, and Minnesota. Thoreau went three times to Maine and to Cape Cod. He climbed many of the mountains in Massachusetts and the surrounding states, but he also traveled away from home for more practical or sentimental reasons. He journeyed to Philadelphia to give a lecture, and he made several excursions to New Bedford to visit his friend Daniel Ricketson. These travels abroad were generally not as satisfying nor as important to Thoreau as were his daily rambles around Concord, but they provided him with variety in his walking.

The significance of Thoreau's walking experience is clear to readers of his *Journal*. Thoreau's *Journal* is the record of his life. Given the quantity and quality of Thoreau's saunterings, it is not surprising that his *Journal* is full of references to his walking experience—references that reveal the paramount role walking played in his life. In fact, walking is perhaps the primary subject and theme of his *Journal*.

It is interesting to observe how many different aspects of Thoreau's walks are touched on in his *Journal* entries. One note recorded for August 19, 1851, depicts the difficulty a walker can have in just leaving the house and commencing a walk: "How many things concur to keep a man at home, to prevent his yielding to his inclination to wander! If I would extend my walk a hundred miles, I must carry a tent on my back for shelter at night or in the rain, or at least I must carry a thick coat to be prepared for a change in the weather. So that it requires some resolution, as well as energy and foresight, to undertake the simplest journey. Man does not travel as easily as the birds migrate. He is not everywhere at home, like flies. When I think how many things I can conveniently carry, I am wont to think it most convenient to stay at home."

In spite of Thoreau's awareness of the difficulties involved with leaving home and walking, he persisted in taking walks. He derived enough satisfaction from his walks to record pleasant memories for the times, especially during the winter, when he could not entertain as many walks: "In the summer we lay up a stock of experiences for the winter, as the squirrel of nuts,—something for conversation in winter evenings. I love to think then of the more distant walks I took in summer."

Thoreau made a careful record in his *Journal* of the daily walking experiences. His journal entries are full of references to the time, conditions, and routes of his walks. No detail seemed too unimportant to record. Typical are these entries: "A clear and pleasant morning. Walked down as far as Moore's at 8 A.M. and returned along the hill"; "9 A.M.—Walk all day with W. E. C., northwest into Acton and Carlisle"; and "I did well to walk in the forenoon, the fresh and inspiring half of this bright day, for now, at mid-afternoon, its brightness is dulled, and a fine stratus is spread over the sky." The direction of the walk interested Thoreau. "There is an advantage in walking eastward these afternoons, at least, that in returning you may have the western sky before you," he noted. Even the temperature merited attention: "When I went to walk it was about 10° above zero, and when I returned, 1°."

Although most of Thoreau's *Journal* descriptions describe daytime perambulations, he also recorded his night walks. One sample entry recounts an evening's ramble to an old house: "We walked up to the old Baker house. In the bright moonlight the character of the ground under our feet was not easy to detect, and we did not know at first but we were walking on sod and not on a field laid down and harrowed." The difficulty of Thoreau's nighttime sauntering emerges in many entries, including this one: "A very dark and stormy night. . . . Where the fence is not painted white I can see nothing, and go whistling for fear I run against some one, though there is little danger that any one will be out. I come against a stone post and bruise my knees; then stumble over a bridge,—being in the gutter. You walk with your hands out to feel the fences and trees. There is no vehicle in the street to-night."

Whether during the night or day, Thoreau's saunterings carried him through many kinds of environments and landscapes. Thoreau learned to anticipate what to expect when venturing into various types of terrain. As a result the *Journal* abounds with such woods-wise observations as this: "You can hardly walk in a thick pine wood now, especially a swamp, but presently you will have a crow or two over your head, either silently flitting over, to spy what you would be at and if its nest is in danger, or angrily cawing."

The tone of Thoreau's descriptions of his walking experience varies as much as did the saunterings themselves. Somber entries like the preceding ones are often balanced in the *Journal* by descriptions that present a lighter touch: "Grasshoppers have been very abundant in dry fields for two or three weeks. Sophia walked through the Depot Field a fortnight ago, and when she got home picked fifty or sixty from her skirts,—for she wore hoops and crinoline. Would not this be a good way to clear a field of them,—to send a bevy of fashionably dressed ladies across a field and leave them to clean their skirts when they got home? It would supplant anything at the patent office, and the motive power is cheap."

As with his humorous side, Thoreau's practical side emerges in several *Journal* depictions of his walks. He records his concern about being sunburned when walking over snow-covered ground and his worry about the dangers posed to the pedestrian by bulls in a pasture. He cautions against sitting underneath white pines in a pine grove "on account of pitch," and he warns about the problems posed by the saunterer making contact with trees that are too heavily laden with snow.

Thoreau's practical approach to walking is most apparent in his interest in the effects of the New England climate on the pedestrian. Thoreau's walking, as with every other New England saunterer, was seasonal, subject to the ever-changing weather patterns with which Concordians were so familiar. Thus his *Journal* records the effects of the extremes of cold and heat, moisture and dryness, to which he found himself exposed during his saunterings: "Walking this afternoon, I notice that the face inclines to stiffen, and the hands and feet get cold soon. On first coming out in very cold weather, I find that I breathe fast, though without walking faster or exerting myself any more than usual"; and "Colder weather, true November weather, comes again to-night, and I must rekindle my fire, which I had done without of late. I must walk briskly in order to keep warm in my thin coat."

Of course Thoreau was sensitive to the effects of snow as well as cold. He disliked hiking on crusty snow, and he found himself frustrated when trying to walk in slushy snow: "I grow so fast and am so weighed down and hindered, that I have to stop continually and look for a rock where I may kick off these newly acquired heels and soles." Thoreau was also bothered by the harsh glare that the snow reflected back into the eyes of the walker. Although he usually found walking in the snow a difficult experience, such was not always the case: "In the early part of winter there was no walking on the snow, but after January, perhaps, when the snow-banks had settled and their surfaces, many times thawed and frozen, become indurated, in fact, you could walk on the snow-crust pretty well."

Many of Thoreau's comments about walking conditions deal with the difficulties of walking after the snow and ice have melted: "It is much worse walking than it has been for ten days, the continual warmth of the sun melting the ice and snow by walls, etc., and reaching the deeper frost, unexpectedly after the surface had been dry. Pastures which look dry prove soft and full of water"; "For the last two or three days very wet and muddy walking, owing to the melting of the snow; which also has slightly swollen the small streams"; and "A thick mist, spiriting away the snow. Very bad walking. . . . The ice is soggy and dangerous to be walked on." Eventually, of course, the ground would dry and the walker's lot would improve: "I walk in the fields now without slumping in the thawing ground, or there are but few soft places, and the distant sand-banks look dry and warm."

Thoreau's *Journal* records his interest in the wind, which brings a welcome dryness to New England in the springtime, but poses new problems to the saunterer who has difficulty maintaining his posture and his dignity against a gale. Conversation in such a wind is nearly impossible, and the sound of the wind running through the water or the trees creates a sense of confusion. "Nevertheless," according to Thoreau, "this universal commotion is very interesting and exciting." These blustery springtime winds can be rather severe, exposing the walker to a winter-like cold when he is least prepared for it: "The 8th, it is clear again, but a very cold and blustering day, yet the wind is worse than the cold. . . . If you must go forth facing the wind, bending to the blast, and sometimes scarcely making any progress, you study how you may return with it on your back. . . . You have no colder walk in winter."

In New England the springtime walker faces not only a stiff wind but rain and mud as well. April showers may bring May flowers, but they also create problems for the saunterer. Thoreau often found walking after a hard rain to be "very bad." He discovered that a "dripping spring rain" makes walking "worse for the time." Damp walking conditions bothered Thoreau, including the "dewy rain" that wet his feet when he traipsed through low lands, and the flooding of the meadows that he waded through. Muddy walking frustrated Thoreau: "Some of the frost has come out, and it is very wet and muddy crossing the plowed fields,—as filthy walking as any in the year. You have the experience of wading birds that get their living on the flats when the tide has gone down and leave their tracks there, but you are cheered by the sight of some radical greenness."

Once the New England saunterer survives springtime wind, rain, and mud, he faces the challenges posed by summer hiking. In his *Journal* Thoreau recorded the heat of summer walking—"Another remarkably warm and pleasant day, if not too hot for walking; 74° at 2 p.m.", and the difficulty of hiking through the thick summer grass that the spring rains had made possible: "Grass now for a week or more has been seriously in the way of the walker, but already I take advantage of the few fields that are mowed. It requires skillful tacking, a good deal of observation, and experience to get across the country now." Inevitably, the dryness of summer posed more difficulties than did the early lush grass. During his summer walks, Thoreau tramped through dust, "several inches deep," which covered his clothes and made walking difficult. But dry conditions allowed Thoreau to walk in places that were normally inaccessible. Thus he hiked through many bogs and swamps in the summertime, although the dryness coupled with the heat could make him feel "as if the ground were on fire, where it was not."

Fall hiking brought relief from summer heat, and Thoreau enjoyed sauntering in the fall. The brisk air, the colorful leaves, and the clear sky invited the New England perambulator to get out into nature and enjoy its beauty. Of particular interest to Thoreau was the experience of walking through fallen leaves. The scent of the leaves—"Leaves now have fairly begun to rustle under foot in wood-paths, especially in chestnut woods, scaring the ducks as you approach the ponds. And what is that common scent there so much like fragrant everlasting?", and the experience of plowing through them—"Now, as you walk in woods, the leaves rustle under your feet as much as ever. In some places you walk pushing a mass before you. In others they half cover pools that are three rods long. They make it slippery climbing hills"—especially impressed Thoreau.

Thoreau's seasonal walking adventure is as carefully recorded, although not as artfully groomed, as is the seasonally organized account of his Walden experience. Thoreau's record of his saunters reveals the very intimate relationship that exists between the saunterer and his environment. Numerous *Journal* entries also demonstrate the consistent daily impact that walking had on Thoreau's life. Like the mailman, Thoreau walked in all kinds of weather, in all kinds of terrain, under all kinds of conditions. And the full extent of that experience is faithfully recorded in the record of his life, his *Journal*.

One cannot help but wonder where Thoreau's interest and acuity in walking came from. What influenced him to become the foremost literary saunterer of his time and to make walking the passion of his life?

Thoreau's parents provided one source for his enthusiasm for walking. Thoreau's mother was a dedicated walker who loved to saunter in nature. She frequently took her children on walks in the surrounding countryside. Actually, both parents walked in nature and took their children with them. But Mrs. Thoreau was probably the more aggressive walker, rumor having it that one of the Thoreau children was nearly born during one of her rambles. Most certainly a love of nature was inculcated in the Thoreau children by their parents as a result of the excursions they all shared.

When Thoreau was quite young, he rambled about the countryside, hunting, trapping, and fishing. He enjoyed this type of primitive contact with nature, but his enjoyment for hunting and fishing was early converted to a love of nature and an interest in natural phenomenon. School took second place. Thanks to the influence of Thoreau's parents, Nature was Thoreau's favorite teacher, and he loved to attend her school. In an early essay, he confesses how, while a student at Harvard, his yearning to walk in nature competed with the pull of the classroom: "Those hours that should have been devoted to study, have been spent in scouring the woods, and exploring the lakes and streams of my native village" ("Autobiography" *Early Essays*).

These early escapes from the rigors of academic life later influenced Thoreau to provide his own pupils with the same experience. When Thoreau was teaching, he frequently took his students on walks. Thoreau's program involved numerous field trips, at least one a week. These excursions introduced his pupils to the history and the natural history of the area. Children loved to walk with Thoreau, and many of them cherished memories of these excursions into their adult years.

One thing that favored Thoreau and his students on their walks was the Concord environment, for Concord was especially well suited for the walker. William Channing describes the suitability of the Concord countryside for the walker in Thoreau's day: "Concord contains an unusual extent of wood and meadow; and the wood-lots, when cut off, are usually continued for the same purpose. So it is a village surrounded by tracts of woodland and meadow, abounding in convenient yet retired paths for walking."

More than family and the local environment, however, influenced Thoreau to commit himself to the walking experience so passionately. One literary work that almost certainly inspired Thoreau to walk outdoors was Ralph Waldo Emerson's *Nature*. Thoreau's conversion from hunter and fisherman to naturalist has been credited to his reading of *Nature*. Thoreau read this book in 1837, and this text infused in him the transcendental fervor that provided the driving force for his excursions.

Yet another influence on Thoreau's walking experience was the travel literature that he read. Influenced by his reading, Thoreau developed his own notions and criteria for the way one ought to travel. He gleaned several pivotal concepts from Goethe, including the importance to the traveler of careful observation, personal involvement, personal growth, and moral stature. From Charles R. Darwin, Thoreau gained a greater appreciation of the value to the traveler "of experiencing (1) the sight of the marvels of natural phenomena, (2) a knowledge of primitive man, (3) contact with the wilderness (vast, unknown, timeless, and so perpetually intriguing), and (4) the appeal of the outdoor, uncivilized, adventurous life" (John Christie, *Thoreau as World Traveler*).

Drawing from his travel reading of Goethe, Darwin, and other travel authors, and tapping his own travel adventures, Thoreau formulated a philosophy of travel that he used to evaluate both his own walking experience and the travels of others. Thoreau envisioned the traveler as a person who combined the qualities of the scientist and the poet—one who studied natural phenomena yet who intuited the value and significance of the observed phenomena. The traveler should be a highly moral individual, and travel should be compatible with his profession.

Perhaps most importantly, one's travel should contribute significantly to personal growth. Thoreau applied his travel philosophy to his own walking experience. His emphasis on observation and intuition, his focus on a serious, primitive, and original approach to nature, and his quest for personal experience and growth shaped the formative nature of his saunterings.

Certainly other things help account for Thoreau's total commitment to sauntering. Perhaps the Concord Lyceum meetings that Thoreau attended furthered his interest in natural history and natural science, two areas he related to his walking experience. But a far more important influence was transcendentalism. Thoreau was, after all, a transcendentalist; and to comprehend adequately the *sans terre* nature of his perambulations and their impact on his life and writings, one needs to consider what there was about transcendentalism that might prefer walking over other modes of travel.

Transcendentalists favored an active life over an inactive one. Many transcendentalists viewed themselves as men of action, and consequently they looked for opportunities to convert their passive, idealistic tenets into physical and mental activity.

Thoreau applied transcendentalism to life by sauntering, a mode of travel very compatible with the transcendental notion of action. Walking offered the individual a more dynamic form of travel than did horse, train, boat, or the other travel modes popular in Thoreau's time. A traveler was more physically and mentally involved with walking than he was with more passive forms of travel that relied on something outside of himself to convey him. Thus walking in nature allowed Thoreau to enjoy the kind of active life to which most transcendentalists aspired.

No activity, however, held value for the transcendentalist unless its outcome or purpose was transcendental in nature. Walking only served the transcendental saunterer when it aided him in his quest to transcend the senses and discover ultimate truths. The productive interplay between the mind and the body during the walking experience enhanced this experience. Walking enabled the walker to directly confront physical nature and to glean its transcendental gems without the encumbrance and interference that other travel forms pose.

Walking offered Thoreau a highly transcendental experience, as this *Journal* entry illustrates: "I take all these walks to every point of the compass, and it is always harvest-time with me. I am always gathering my crop from these woods and fields and waters, and no man is in my way or interferes with me. My crop is not their crop. . . . The farmer has always come to the field after some material thing; that is not what a philosopher goes there for."

Only when Thoreau had exhausted the transcendental potential of the walking experience could he think of other things: "Ah! When a man has travelled, and robbed the horizon of his native fields of its mystery and poetry, its indefinite promise, tarnished the blue of distant mountains with his feet! When he has done this he may begin to think of another world. What is this longer to him?"

The democratic nature of transcendentalism also favored walking as a form of travel. Transcendentalists believed that each individual possessed within himself unlimited potential for spiritual growth and self-fulfillment. This made all men equal before God.

When this theory of democracy was applied to types of transportation, walking proved the most democratic mode available to the transcendentalist. Anyone can walk, anywhere, anytime, without cost. Walking caters to no particular class or party; it allows the individual saunterer to realize his full potential. When Thoreau walked, he walked as an American, one who could, like the famous celebrator of democracy, Walt Whitman, follow his intuitions at will.

This notion of following one's intuitions was central to transcendental thinking, and an understanding of it is important to interpreting Thoreau's sauntering experience. According to Emerson, "Every man discriminates between the voluntary acts of his mind and his involuntary perceptions, and knows that to his involuntary perceptions a perfect faith is due" ("Self-Reliance" *Works* 2:65). In *Walden* Thoreau makes this claim: "If one listens to the faintest but constant suggestions of his genius, which are certainly true, he sees not to what extremes, or even insanity, it may lead him; and yet that way, as he grows more resolute and faithful, his road lies."

Following one's good genius not only leads a person to the road he should travel, it also strengthens his individuality and creates a strong self-sufficiency, two traits very common to Americans in general, and to walkers in particular. Transcendentalists were strong individualists. Emerson's admonition "Trust thyself: every heart vibrates to that iron string" ("Self-Reliance" *Works*) was the credo of transcendentalism. Self-sufficiency governed every aspect of the transcendentalist's life.

Walking is the best transportation mode for nurturing one's individuality and self-reliance. It frees the traveler more than other types of transportation do to follow the dictates of his intuition. Therefore, walking allowed Thoreau a measure of freedom that he did not experience with other travel modes. For example, when Thoreau compared foot travel with horse travel, he concluded: "It is far more independent to travel on foot. You have to sacrifice so much to the horse."

In Thoreau's time the most popular transportation forms were horseback, train, canal boat, and carriages. But these public forms of transportation offered a transcendentalist like Thoreau very little in terms of private, meditative, and individualistic experience. Thoreau availed himself of all the transportation forms of his day when necessary, including railroad and steamboat travel, yet he considered walking the best model of travel. That he thought walking a superior form of transportation to travel by rail is evident in *Walden*, where he writes: "One says to me, 'I wonder that you do not lay up money; you love to travel; you might take the cars and go to Fitchburg to-day and see the country.' But I am wiser than that. I have learned that the swiftest traveller is he that goes afoot. I say to my friend, Suppose we try who will get there first. The distance is thirty miles; the fare ninety cents. That is almost a day's wages. . . . Well, I start now on foot, and get there before night; I have travelled at that rate by the week together. You will in the mean while have earned your fare, and arrive there some time to-morrow, or possibly this evening, if you are lucky enough to get a job in season. . . . And so, if the railroad reached round the world, I think that I should keep ahead of you; and as for seeing the country and getting experience of that kind, I should have to cut your acquaintance altogether."

Although Thoreau frequently boated in the summertime and ice-skated in winter, he was consistent during all seasons in his dedication to walking and the independence it granted him. One contemporary of Thoreau's recalls inviting Thoreau to come and see him in Vermont. "I began to tell him," he recounts, "how he could get to Vermont, and he said, 'Oh, I sha'n't go by rail, I shall take a bee line and walk'" (Wood). When Thoreau, traveling by train to visit his friend Bronson Alcott, discovered that the train would be delayed for three-and-a-half hours, he hiked five miles to the next station rather than waiting for the train to leave. Thoreau's fiercely independent spirit was nurtured in true transcendental fashion by his sauntering experience. Walking allowed Thoreau to go where he wanted to go and do what he wanted to do wherever and whenever he wanted to.

Nonconformity was a key aspect of the independent

nature of Thoreau's walking experience. When praising the transcendental virtues of nonconformity, Emerson stated, "We will walk on our own feet; we will work with our own hands; we will speak our own minds" ("The American Scholar" *Works*); and Thoreau reveled in the nonconformist nature of the walking experience. One walker has noted: "There is no orthodoxy in walking. It is a land of many paths and no-paths, where every one goes his own way and is right" (Trevelyan). Thoreau rebelled against conformity in any form, including conformity in the walking experience, which he insisted be original and natural: "When I hear the hypercritical quarrelling about grammar and style, the position of the particles, etc., etc., stretching or contracting every speaker to certain rules of theirs,—Mr. Webster, perhaps, not having spoken according to Mr. Kirkham's rule,—I see that they forget that the first requisite and rule is that expression shall be vital and natural, as much as the voice of a brute or an interjection. . . . The grammarian is often one who can neither cry nor laugh, yet thinks that he can express human emotions. So the posture—masters tell you how you shall walk,—turning your toes out, perhaps, excessively,—but so the beautiful walkers are not made."

For transcendentalists, walking was both a democratic, individualistic enterprise and a patriotic act. Transcendentalism advocated a break with the United States's cultural ties to Europe; transcendentalists preached the superiority of the American landscape and the virtuous influence of that landscape on those, like walkers, who enjoyed a direct relationship with the American wilderness. Emerson made this clear when he asserted in "The Young American," "The land is the appointed remedy for whatever is false and fantastic in our culture. The continent we inhabit is to be physic and food for our mind, as well as our body" (*Works*). In the same essay Emerson elaborated on the patriotic nature of relating to the American landscape:

Any relation to the land, the habit of tilling it, or mining it, or even hunting on it, generates the feeling of patriotism. The vast majority of the people of this country live by the land, and carry its quality in their manners and opinions. . . . I think we must regard the land as a commanding and increasing power on the citizen, the sanative and Americanizing influence, which promises to disclose new virtues for ages to come.

Thoreau freely praised the superiority of the American landscape in "Walking": "If the moon looks larger here than in Europe, probably the sun looks larger also. If the heavens of America appear infinitely higher, and the stars brighter, I trust that these facts are symbolical of the height to which the philosophy and poetry and religion of her inhabitants may one day soar."

So strong was Thoreau's patriotism when walking, that his one sauntering excursion outside the United States, his trip to Canada, proved unsatisfactory. Thoreau's literary account of this trip contains considerable humor— "the result of the irreverence bred of his feeling of American superiority" (Paul). The political and cultural differences of Canada made it impossible for him to enjoy or profit from his walking experience. Thoreau remained at heart an American walker.

The transcendentalist's advocacy of a nonmaterialistic society also favored the American walking experience. Transcendentalists found Americans too materialistic, and they valued activities like walking that affirmed the participant's economic and spiritual integrity. In "Self-Reliance" R. W. Emerson expressed his regret over forms of material progress that hamper the walking experience:

"The civilized man has built a coach, but has lost the use of his feet. He is supported on crutches, but lacks so much support of muscle." In his essay on Thoreau he praised the economical efficiency of Thoreau's walking experience: "He chose to be rich by making his wants few, and supplying them himself. In his travels, he used the railroad only to get over so much country as was unimportant to the present purpose, walking hundreds of miles, avoiding taverns, buying a lodging in farmers' and fishermen's houses, as cheaper, and more agreeable to him, and because there he could better find the men and the information he wanted" ("Thoreau").

For Thoreau, the value of a walk was determined, in part, by the naturalness and simplicity of the experience. Luxurious forms of travel did not appeal to him—a point he makes in *Walden:* "I would rather sit on a pumpkin and have it all to myself, than be crowded on a velvet cushion. I would rather ride on earth in an ox cart with a free circulation, than go to heaven in the fancy car of an excursion train and breathe a *malaria* all the way."

In their thinking and in their actions, transcendentalists attempted to simplify life, to reduce its complexities to a manageable condition. In *Walden* Thoreau urged others to "simplify, simplify." He argued that the only cure for the artificial complexities of American life was "a Spartan simplicity."

Thoreau favored walking because it was natural and uncomplicated. He had no tolerance for cumbersome approaches to the travel experience: "They are hopelessly cockneys everywhere who learn to swim with a machine. They take neither disease nor health, nay, nor life itself, the natural way. I see dumbbells in the minister's study, and some of their dumbness gets into his sermons. Some travellers carry them round the world in their carpetbags. . . . I cannot be interested in these extremely artificial amusements. The traveller is no longer a wayfarer, with his staff and pack and dusty coat. His is not a pilgrim, but he travels in a saloon, and carries dumb-bells to exercise with in the intervals of his journey."

When Thoreau walked he sauntered in true transcendental fashion, gleaning transcendental insights from his journeys and applying transcendental beliefs in simplicity, independence, patriotism, and naturalness to his perambulations.

Regardless of external influences like transcendentalism that might be traced to explain Thoreau's walking experience, his own personality influenced him most. Something within Thoreau dictated that he would be a walker. The act of walking freed his "self" and affirmed his identity.

Thoreau had a built-in need to walk; his metabolism and personal chemistry required it. This need to walk was most apparent when ill health prevented him from walking. In his "Journals" Bronson Alcott recorded such a time, connecting Thoreau's deterioration to his inability to saunter: "Channing writes tenderly of Thoreau's confinement, and I see him this morning and find his hoarseness forbids his going out as usual. 'Tis a serious thing to one who has been less a house-keeper than any man in town, has lived out of doors for the best part of his life, has harvested more wind and storm, sun and sky, and has more weather in him, than any—. . . . Fair weather and spring time, I trust, are to prove his best physicians, and the woods and fields know their old friend again presently."

Sauntering was in Thoreau's blood. In *Cape Cod* he wrote that it would take more than "two good drying days to cure [him] of rambling." In his *Journal* he mentions how "accustomed to a roaming field-life" he was, and the "muscular irritability" he experienced whenever he was deprived of walking experience. Thoreau walked so frequently, and his body was so used to the stimulation of a walk, that being unable to walk created a tremendous amount of pent-up psychological and physical energy. A contemporary of Thoreau's recalls one time when Thoreau had not taken his customary walk. He flew down from upstairs and commenced an enthusiastic and uncharacteristic dance, much to the amusement of all who were present (Anonymous, "Reminiscences of Thoreau," in Harding, *Thoreau: Man of Concord*).

Thoreau's walks were necessary for his emotional, intellectual, and physical well-being. In his *Journal* Thoreau acknowledged his need to "be out-of-doors enough to get experience of wholesome reality, as a ballast to thought and sentiment. Health requires this relaxation, this aimless life. This life in the present. Let a man have thought what he will of Nature in the house, she will still be novel outdoors." He added, "I keep out of doors for the sake of the mineral, vegetable, and animal in me."

When Thoreau satisfied his built-in need to walk, his personality emerged. This is not surprising since, according to Sussman and Goode, walking styles usually reveal much about the individual walker: "We walk differently at different times, and the way we walk at any given moment expresses our state of mind and emotion at that moment, our content or discontent, our drive and purposefulness or our timidity, languor, indifference, despair. A walking style unmasks the feelings in all their nuances.

But it unmasks much more. It expresses our whole physical and psychological history. A habitual walking style reveals with great accuracy the individual's deepest attitudes toward the world and toward himself, attitudes of which he himself may be unaware. To those who have eyes to see and empathy to feel with him, his walk tells what he is and what he has been."

Aware of this relationship between walking style and personality, Thoreau liked to classify and analyze people by their walk: "Why do laborers so commonly turn out their feet more than the class still called gentlemen, apparently pushing themselves along by the sides of their feet? I think you can tell the track of a clown from that of a gentleman, though he should wear a gentleman's boots." The relationship between a man's walk and his identity fascinated Thoreau: "Coming home last night in the twilight, I recognized a neighbor a dozen rods off by his walk or carriage, though it was so dark that I could not see a single feature of his person. . . . It was because the man within the clothes moved them in a peculiar manner that I knew him thus at once at a distance and in the twilight. He made a certain figure in any clothes he might wear, and moved in it in a peculiar manner. Indeed, we have a very intimate knowledge of one another; we see through thick and thin; spirit meets spirit. A man hangs out innumerable signs by which we may know him."

Thoreau's own walking stride epitomized his direct approach to life. E. W. Emerson remembered Thoreau's gait this way: "When he walked to get over the ground one thought of a tireless machine, seeing his long, direct, uniform pace; but his body was active and well balanced, and his step could be light, as of one who could leap or dance or skate well at will." Some noted that when Thoreau walked, he looked directly ahead yet had an Indian-like ability to observe everything. Others recorded that Thoreau's determined stride was like that of a soldier. However differently Thoreau's walk struck people, all agreed that its no-nonsense, direct approach matched his strident personality and confrontational approach to life. One could know much about Thoreau just by watching him march down the streets of Concord or saunter in the woods.

One personality trait—his particularity—was especially evident in Thoreau's walking. He had strong feelings about how the walker should go about the walk itself; details were important. Mary Hosmer Brown, a contemporary of Thoreau's, recounted that "to take a walk with Thoreau, one must rigidly adhere to the manners of the woods." Thoreau could not tolerate walking with someone who would not be quiet and still when the situation called for it.

The amount of vigor the walker employed was also important to Thoreau. Walking should be a buoyant, enthusiastic experience: "There must be respiration as well as aspiration—We should not walk on tiptoe, but healthily expand to our full circumference on the soles of our feet"; and the walker's stride should match the fervor of his spirit: "Every time he steps buoyantly up—he steps solidly down again, and stands the firmer on the ground for his independence upon it. We should fetch the whole-heel-sole-and toe—horizontally down to earth" (*Journal* [Princeton]). The walker's posture also concerned Thoreau, who thought that "a man should be collected and earnest in his bearing—moving like one and not several, like an arrow with a feather for its rudder—and not like a handful of feathers bound to a rod,—or a disorderly equipage which does not move unanimously" (*Journal* [Princeton]). Even the walking pace deserves attention. Just as "nature never makes haste," the saunterer should avoid undue hurry, pacing himself with the rhythms of nature. "The wise man abides there where he is, as some walkers actually rest the whole body at each step, while others never relax the muscles of the leg till the accumulated fatigue obliges them to stop short" (*Journal* [Princeton]).

Thoreau was even particular about the walker's clothing and equipment. Thoreau's utilitarian approach to dressing and outfitting for a journey was compatible with his no-frills approach to life.

Thoreau often wore a clay-colored pair of corduroy trousers, which not only helped him blend in with his surroundings but also required less cleaning. Thoreau's friends disapproved of his plain walking attire, but this did not bother him in the least. Thoreau writes in *Walden* that clothing serves man by keeping him warm and covering his nakedness. He believed that clothing becomes so assimilated with the wearer's own character that he hesitates to part with it when it is worn and old. Patches and worn clothing are often evidences of a strong character, and new enterprises call, not for new clothes, but new wearers of clothes. "If you have any enterprise before you, try it in your old clothes."

In "A Yankee in Canada" Thoreau discusses his commitment to dressing and traveling practically: "I never wear my best coat on a journey, though perchance I could show a certificate to prove that I have a more costly one, at least, at home, if that were all that a gentleman required. It is not wise for a traveler to go dressed. . . . Honest traveling is about as dirty work as you can do, and a man needs a pair of overalls for it. As for blacking my shoes in such a case, I should as soon think of blacking my face."

A walker, of course, pays special attention to his boots and shoes. Thoreau gave considerable thought to his footwear, especially in wintertime. He matched his winter footwear to the different conditions that he faced: "It becomes quite a study how a man will shoe himself for a winter. For outdoor life in winter, I use three kinds of shoes or boots: first and chiefly, for the ordinary dry snows or bare ground, cowhide boots; secondly, for shallow thaws, half-shoe depth, and spring weather, light boots and india-rubbers; third, for the worst sloshy weather, about a week in the year, india-rubber boots." Thoreau wore boots to protect himself from being cut by meadow grass, and he wore them to "wade through the shallow water where [frogs] were found."

Thoreau knew firsthand the footwear needs of the

naturalist, and shoddy bootmaking or improper walking upset him. He complained that most men, when walking in the outdoors, "ignore the worlds above and below, keep straight along, and do not run their boots down at the heel as I do. How to keep the heels up I have been obliged to study carefully, turning the nigh foot painfully on side-hills." Unforgivable were the shoemakers who, "to save a few iron heel-pegs, do not complete the rows on the inside by three or four,—the very place in the whole boot where they are most needed,—which has fatal consequences to the buyer. . . . It is as if you put no underpinning under one corner of your house." Thoreau equipped himself with sturdy boots, and he was proud of the fact that by walking properly he could "cross very wet and miry places dry-shod by moving rapidly on [his] heels."

Thoreau even wrote in his *Journal* about shoestrings and laces and the best ways to tie them: "I always use leather strings tied in a hard knot; they untie but too easily even then." Thoreau's frustration with keeping his shoes tied led to this humorous but informative commentary: "I have for years had a great deal of trouble with my shoe-strings, because they get untied continually. They are leather, rolled and tied in a hard knot. But some days I could hardly go twenty rods before I was obliged to stop and stoop to tie my shoes. My companion and I speculated on the distance to which one tying would carry you,—the length of a shoe-tie,—and we thought it nearly as appreciable and certainly a more simple and natural measure of distance than a stadium, or league, or mile. Ever and anon we raised our feet on whatever fence or wall or rock or stump we chanced to be passing, and drew the strings once more, pulling as hard as we could. It was very vexatious, when passing through low scrubby bushes, to become conscious that the strings were already getting lose again before we had fairly started.

What would we have done if pursued by a tribe of Indians?"

Thoreau attempted several things to solve this pesky problem, although he did not go as far as his companion who tried walking without any shoestrings at all—too "loose" a procedure for Thoreau. Thoreau purchased special shoestrings "made of the hide of a South American jackass," but these were no better than his other ones. He "thought of strings with recurved prickles and various other remedies," all to no avail. Finally, experimenting with knot tying, he mastered the square knot and tied his shoes so well that his only difficulty was in untying them. He thought that all children should be taught this knot. So rigorous was Thoreau's walking, that this square knot needed "to be as secure as a reef-knot in any gale, to withstand the wringing and twisting" that resulted from his walks.

Thoreau believed that no walker should venture forth ill equipped. He advocated traveling light but practically. In "A Yankee in Canada" he mentions that he kept a "list of those articles which, from frequent experience, [he] found indispensable to the foot-traveler." Whenever he prepared to travel on a lengthy journey, he would consult this list. Thoreau's list included a handkerchief for carrying things in and an umbrella. He considered himself a knight of the umbrella and the bundle, and he disdained anyone who traveled with excess baggage: "Even the elephant carries but a small trunk on his journeys. The perfection of traveling is to travel without baggage."

Thoreau's walking revealed another of his key traits— perseverance. Although Thoreau was short and ungainly, he had the stamina needed to undertake the most arduous walks. William Channing described his friend this way: "He [Thoreau] was known among the lads of his age as one who did not fear mud or water, nor paused to lift his followers over a ditch. So in his later journeys, if his companion was footsore and loitered, he steadily pursued the road, making his strength self-serviceable. . . . That wildness that in him nothing could subdue still lay beneath his culture. Once when a follower was done up with headache and incapable of motion, hoping his associate would comfort him and perhaps afford him a sip of tea, he said, 'There are people who are sick in that way every morning, and go about their affairs,' and then marched off about his. In such limits, so inevitable, was he compacted."

Thoreau was proud of his tenacity and recorded in his *Journal* Channing's admiration of it: "C. [Channing] kept up an incessant strain of wit, banter, about my legs, which were so springy and unweariable, declared I had got my double legs on, that they were not cork but steel, that I should . . . have sent them to the World's Fair."

Walking was an activity well suited to Thoreau's personality. It freed his transcendental side, allowing him independence and freedom, and catered to his utilitarian side, channeling his practicality, particularity, and determination.

Walking was a daily, integral part of Thoreau's unique approach to life. It was the vehicle by which he sought to front the cosmos and discover ultimate truth. The assertion that Thoreau's walks "were the source and structure of all he wished to be, to know, and to write about" (Fussell) appropriately emphasizes—as does Thoreau's own *Journal* record—the central and formative nature of Thoreau's sauntering. Paired with his transcendental beliefs and unique personality, walking offered Thoreau the most desirable form of travel. He walked as often as he could, soberly dedicating himself to the sauntering life.

2

EXPLORING THE MICROCOSM

Thoreau once reflected: "If these fields and streams and woods, the phenomena of nature here, and the simple occupations of the inhabitants should cease to interest and inspire me, no culture or wealth would atone for the loss." Each day Thoreau's life pulsed in wonder at the world around him. Driven by an insatiable, childlike curiosity, he sauntered forth to explore the mysteries of life.

In the *Maine Woods* Thoreau expresses his faith in the inexhaustible potential of the American landscape: "I am reminded by my journey how exceedingly new this country is. You have only to travel for a few days into the interior and back parts even of many of the old states, to come to that very America which the Northmen, and Cabot, and Gosnold, and Smith and Raleigh visited. If Columbus was the first to discover the islands, Americus Vespucius, and Cabot, and the Puritans, and we their descendants, have discovered only the shores of America. While the republic has already acquired a history worldwide, America is still unsettled and unexplored."

When Thoreau considered the landscape around him, he sensed the exciting potential for walkers like himself who, although they lived in the wake of the original explorers, could still make their own discoveries. The early adventurers had left plenty for others to explore: "We have advanced by leaps to the Pacific, and left many a lesser Oregon and California unexplored behind us."

In *Walden* Thoreau writes that "village life would stagnate if it were not for the unexplored forests and meadows which surround it," and he felt that most of his contemporaries were slow to sense the possibilities of discovery in their environment and experiences. While Thoreau sauntered, ferreting out the secrets of nature, his townsmen sat on their porches "practising idle and musty virtues." While Thoreau responded to the "incessant influx of novelty into the world," his countrymen tolerated "incredible dulness."

One of the most important and interesting aspects of Thoreau's sauntering explorations is the preparation he made for many of his walks. Most of Thoreau's walks were calculated adventures intended to produce rewarding discoveries. When he prepared for serious hiking, Thoreau was meticulous about his clothing and his equipment. Channing, Thoreau's most faithful walking companion, provides this description of Thoreau's careful preparation: "Before he set out on a foot journey, he collected every information as to the routes and the place to which he was going, through the maps and guidebooks. . . . His route being known, he made a list of all he should carry,—the sewing materials never forgotten (as he was a vigorous walker, and did not stick at a hedge more than an English racer), the pounds of bread, the sugar, salt, and tea carefully decided on. . . . With him the botany must go too, and the book for pressing flowers . . . , and the guide-book, spy-glass, and measuring-tape."

Thoreau was convinced that careful preparation would help a saunterer avoid unnecessary distractions and pitfalls. He advised: "I should say: Never undertake to ascend a mountain or thread a wilderness where there is any danger of being lost, without taking thick clothing, partly india-rubber, if not a tent or material for one; the best map to be had and a compass; salt pork and hard-bread and salt; fish-hooks and lines; a good jack-knife, at least, if not a hatchet, and perhaps a gun; matches in a vial stopped water-tight; some strings and paper. Do not take a dozen steps which you could not with tolerable accuracy protract on a chart."

Preparation was a principle with Thoreau. In actual practice he was not always so careful to follow a map or avoid getting lost as he would lead the reader to think, but he did believe in the paramount importance of being adequately prepared, especially if the walk was to take place in unfamiliar or dangerous territory.

Before each walk Thoreau assembled the equipment he would need. Much of this equipment, such as a botany book and book for pressing flowers, were a consistent part of Thoreau's walks. But he could improvise when necessary. His use of a hat to preserve botany finds inspired this *Journal* commentary: "I am inclined to think that my hat, whose lining is gathered in midway so as to make a shelf, is about as good a botany-box as I could have and far more convenient, and there is something in the darkness and the vapors that arise from the head—at least if you take a bath—which preserves the flowers through a long walk."

Physical and material readiness were important to Thoreau, but mental preparation was even more crucial. In *Cape Cod* Thoreau reveals his understanding that the explorer's attitude often determines the exploration outcome: "The heroes and discoverers have found true more than was previously believed, only when they were expecting and dreaming of something more than their contemporaries dreamed of, or even themselves discovered, that is, when they were in a frame of mind fitted to behold the truth."

Thoreau discovered what he mentally prepared himself to discover. His own powers of suggestion yielded concrete fruits in Nature's vineyard: "We may detect that some sort of preparation and faint expectation preceded every discovery we have made. We blunder into no discovery but it will appear that we have prayed and disciplined ourselves for it." Time and again Thoreau experienced the fulfillment of his expectations: "It commonly chances that I make my most interesting botanical discoveries when I [am] in a thrilled and expectant mood, perhaps wading in some remote swamp where I have just found something novel and feel more than usually remote from the town. Or some rare plant which for some reason has occupied a strangely prominent place in my thoughts for some time will present itself. My expectation ripens to discovery. I am prepared for strange things."

Thoreau's saunterings exemplify the concept of mind over matter. In typical transcendental fashion, the saunterer's good genius controls his senses and leads him to the quarry he seeks. When the inner image fails, the external stimulus fails as well. The inner picture must be attuned to the outer one for the walker to make the discovery he seeks: "We cannot see anything until we are possessed with the idea of it, and then we can hardly see anything else. In my botanical rambles I find that first the idea, or image, of a plant occupies my thoughts, though it may at first seem very foreign to this locality, and for some weeks or months I go thinking of it and expecting it unconsciously, and at length I surely see it, and it is henceforth an actual neighbor of mine. This is the history of my finding a score or more of rare plants which I could name."

In "Autumnal Tints" Thoreau observes how we fail to see things "because we do not bring our minds and eyes to bear on them; for there is no power to see in the eye itself, any more than in any other jelly."

Thoreau's exploratory process contrasts sharply with

the existential conundrum described by Martin Heidegger. Thoreau sought the concrete manifestations of nature, but modern man, according to Heidegger, seeks "nothing." If, as Thoreau and Heidegger both maintain, man will only discover what he anticipates, one dilemma for the modern explorer is how to anticipate "nothing" in order to discover it. Thoreau could envision the discovery of a plant or other concrete reality, but how does one expect to find "nothing"? This problem fascinated Heidegger: "Where shall we seek the nothing? Where will we find the nothing? In order to find something must we not already know in general that it is there? Indeed! At first and for the most part man can seek only when he has anticipated the being at hand of what he is looking for. Now the nothing is what we are seeking. Is there ultimately such a thing as a search without that anticipation, a search to which pure discovery belongs?"

Thoreau, of course, faced no such difficulty. As a nineteenth-century explorer, he sought to discover concrete phenomena; the abstract "nothing" to which Heidegger refers did not interest Thoreau.

Important to Thoreau's process of anticipation was an adept sense of timing. He could anticipate when and where to walk in order to make the discoveries he sought: "A man must attend to Nature closely for many years to know when, as well as where, to look for his objects, since he must always anticipate her a little. . . . I would know when in the year to expect certain thoughts and moods, as the sportsman knows when to look for plover."

With expectations based upon time and place, the walker roves through Nature, his sauntering eye alert to the images in his head. His focused perspective allows him to see what others might not see, to discover what others might miss. After observing a bird during one of his rambles, Thoreau noted: "At length the walker who sits meditating on a distant bank sees the little dipper sail out from amid the weeds and busily dive for its food along their edge. Yet ordinary eyes might range up and down the river all day and never detect its small black head above the water."

With anticipation and a proper perspective, Thoreau set out on his walks to discover Nature. His walks became an extension of his visual projection of them. Much like planning a dream and then dreaming it, Thoreau anticipated his walking adventures and then lived them out. Using this process Thoreau discovered things as varied as plants ("It is a remarkable fact that, in the case of the most interesting plants which I have discovered in this vicinity, I have anticipated finding them perhaps a year before the discovery") and artifacts ("I never find a remarkable Indian relic—I find a good many—but I have first divined its existence, and planned the discovery of it. Frequently I have told myself distinctly what it was to be before I found it").

Not all of Thoreau's exploratory rambles, however, were carefully planned, nor were all of his discoveries clearly anticipated. Some walks were extemporaneous, and, because of his boy-like wonder, Thoreau experienced great joy when these spontaneous walks led him to sudden and unexpected discoveries. He revelled in the ecstasy derived from his own unexpected finds: "No man ever makes a discovery, ever an observation of the least importance, but he is advertised of the fact by a joy that surprises him. The powers thus celebrate all discovery." He could not "conceive of anything so surprising and thrilling but that something more surprising may be actually presented to us."

Thoreau's writings contain a number of references to unexpected discoveries made during his saunterings. These finds, made possible by the extended reach of his walks, filled his life with a special and intense exuberance. After one walk during which he had suddenly come across a particular plant, he recorded in his *Journal:* "How sweet is the perception of a new natural fact! suggesting what worlds remain to be unveiled. That phenomenon of the andromeda seen against the sun cheers me exceedingly. . . . It makes all those parts of the country where it grows more attractive and elysian to me. It is a natural magic. These little leaves are the stained windows in the cathedral of my world. At sight of any redness I am excited like a cow."

Thoreau's response to finding some phosphorescent wood during an excursion in the Maine woods proved equally exciting: "I was exceedingly interested by this phenomenon, and already felt paid for my journey. It could hardly have thrilled me more if it had taken the form of letters, or of the human face. . . . I little thought that there was such light shining in the darkness of the wilderness for me" (*Maine Woods*).

The act of walking made such discoveries seem all the more unexpected. The saunterer could travel through thick woods, unaware of what might be on the other side. Just turning a corner or reaching the other side of a woods might yield an unforeseen prospect: "Crouching you thread your way amid some dense shrub oak wood some day, descending next through the almost impenetrable hedge, and stand to your surprise on the edge of this fair open meadow with a bottom of unfathomed mud, as retired and novel as if it were a thousand miles removed from your ordinary walks."

Thoreau's sudden discovery of berry patches along a road evoked a similar reaction: "I seem to have wandered into a land of greater fertility, some up-country Eden. Are not these the delectable hills? It is a land flowing with milk and honey. Great shining blackberries peep out at me from under the leaves upon the rocks." Unexpected discoveries transported Thoreau to his own private paradise.

Thoreau attempted to take in all of Nature's manifestations; he comprehensively surveyed and studied its many features and secrets. The more he explored Nature, the more ambitious his explorations became, as this *Journal* entry demonstrates: "I soon found myself observing when plants first blossomed and leafed, and I followed it up early and late, far and near, several years in succession, running to different sides of the town and into the neighboring towns, often between twenty and thirty miles in a day. I often visited a particular plant four or five miles distant, half a dozen times within a fortnight, that I might know exactly when it opened, beside attending to a great many others in different directions and some of them equally distant, at the same time. At the same time I had an eye for birds and whatever else might offer." Such a commitment to studying every feature of the landscape led to the comprehensiveness of Thoreau's walking experience as his walks attempted to keep pace with his insatiable curiosity.

Walking allowed Thoreau to explore thoroughly the Concord countryside. He walked everywhere and observed everything that he could. His search knew no bounds, as John Burroughs, a naturalist and contemporary of Thoreau's, makes clear: "He shadowed every flower and bird and musquash that appeared. His vigilance was unceasing; not a mouse or a squirrel must leave its den without his knowledge. . . . He was up in the morning and off to some favorite haunt earlier than the day-laborers; and he chronicled his observations on the spot, as if the case was to be tried in court the next day and he was the principal witness. He watched the approach of spring as a doctor watches the development of a critical case. He felt the pulse of the wind and the temperature of the day at all hours. He examined the plants growing under water, and noted the radical leaves of various weeds that keep green all winter under snow. . . . The first sight of bare ground and of the red earth excited him. The fresh meadow spring odor was to him like the fragrance of tea to an old tea-drinker." Walking aided Thoreau's explorations in several ways. Walking made it easier for Thoreau to record his field observations. Thoreau's *Journal* is permeated with entries based on his field notes. Walking allowed him to write down any observation at the moment. He could study a particular phenomenon and record it without interruption or inconvenience. The immediacy and force of many of Thoreau's *Journal* entries is attributable to these notes, which carry the impact of the moment of truth or insight with which they are associated.

In much the same way, walking aided Thoreau when he collected specimens for further study. It allowed him to collect and carry many different objects for further study. Channing notes that Thoreau's large pockets proved ample for most prizes, and, excepting very large objects, he would carry home with him "objects of all kinds,—pieces of wood or stone, lichens, seeds, nuts, apples, or whatever he had found for his uses. For he was a vigorous collector, never omitting to get and keep every possible thing in his direction of study." During his saunterings, Thoreau collected whatever was valuable to him, regardless of the value others placed on such things: "What I put into my pocket, whether berry or apple, generally has to keep company with an arrowhead or two. . . . These are the perennial crop of Concord fields. If they were sure it would pay, we should see farmers raking the fields for them."

Walking was especially useful in helping Thoreau probe every surface feature of the landscape. His feet splashed through the water and trudged through the mud of swamps and meadows; they stirred the dust of roads, sauntered through the pine needles of the forest, and climbed the rocks of mountains. Thoreau explored every aspect of the various surfaces that the walker could study in the Concord area: "It is a certain faeryland where we live. You may walk out in any direction over the earth's surface, lifting your horizon, and everywhere your path, climbing the convexity of the globe, leads you between heaven and earth."

Thoreau's walks frequently carried him to water or to the water's edge. Thoreau often sloshed through flooded meadows or swampy areas. During one meadow jaunt he explored a small hole that proved to be the nest of a fish. He picked the fish up and examined it. After releasing it he felt with his hand for the fish's eggs, which lay in the mud. The discovery is described in his *Journal:* "Pouts, then, make their nests in shallow mud-holes or bays, in masses of weedy mud, or probably in the muddy bank; and the old pout hovers over the spawn or keeps guard at the entrance."

Thoreau enjoyed exploring water life in the Concord area: "I walk these days along the brooks, looking for tortoises and trout, etc. They are full of a rust-colored water, as if they flowed out of an iron mine." R. W. Emerson remembered the many times that Thoreau waded into pools searching for water plants. Emerson was struck by the way that Thoreau would discover a plant and, while standing in the middle of the pool, pull his notes out of his pocket to check on when the plant should bloom. At the same time Thoreau listened to bird calls and identified birds.

Walking also helped Thoreau trace the movements of water animals that had left their imprints behind: "Walking over the river meadows to examine the pools and see how much dried up they are, I notice, as usual, the track of the musquash, some five inches wide always, always exactly in the lowest part of the muddy hollows connecting one pool with another, winding as they wind, as if loath to raise itself above the lowest mud."

Thoreau studied the distinguishing features of swamps and meadows. In one November *Journal* entry he records that he "walked through Gowing's Swamp from west to east." He then classifies the three main portions of the swamp that his walk revealed—"first, the thin woody; second, the coarse bushy or gray; and third, the fine bushy or brown." He discusses the features of each of these areas of the swamp, including the kinds of trees that surround the swamp, the "very bad thicket" that makes walking difficult as one draws nearer the center of the swamp, and "the smooth brown and wetter spaces," including the "open pool" that comprise the heart of the swamp.

Thoreau's final view of the swamp results from climbing the "high land on the south," from which he "looked down over the large open space with its *navel* pool in the centre." He notes that the swamp appears to have no "natural outlet, though an artificial one has been dug." Only walking could have made possible such a thorough examination of such difficult terrain.

Thoreau's walking bridged the surfaces of land and water. Walking allowed him to explore freely the phenomena of both environments. When Thoreau wrote his sister, Helen, in July 1843, he informed her that he had explored inland and along the shore of Long Island, where he was staying. Thoreau explored the land and the shore wherever he traveled, always conscious of the distinctive surface features that he observed.

Thoreau's fascination with the blending of the land and the water is most apparent in his Cape Cod experience. When he hiked the sand-bank that separated the Cape Cod beach from the rest of the land, he was awed by the magical combination of the beach and ocean with the sandy terrain inland. He recorded the view with near reverence: "This sand-bank—the backbone of the Cape—rose directly from the beach to the height of a hundred feet or more above the ocean. It was with singular emotions that we first stood upon it and discovered what a place we had chosen to walk on. On our right, beneath us, was the beach of smooth and gently-sloping sand, a dozen rods in width; next, the endless series of white breakers; further still, the light green water over the bar, which runs the whole length of the forearm of the Cape, and beyond this stretched the unwearied and illimitable ocean. On our left, extending back from the very edge of the bank, was a perfect desert of shining sand, from thirty to eighty rods in width, skirted in the distance by small sand-hills fifteen or twenty feet high; between which, however, in some places, the sand penetrated as much farther. Next commenced the region of vegetation."

The sand-bank he traversed reminded Thoreau of "the escarped rampart of a stupendous fortress, whose glacis was the beach, and whose champaign the ocean. . . . In short," he felt himself "traversing a desert, with the view of an autumnal landscape of extraordinary brilliancy, a sort of Promised Land, on the one hand, and the ocean on the other." Here was a landscape that isolated and overshadowed the traveler: "The solitude was that of the ocean and the desert combined. A thousand men could not have seriously interrupted it, but would have been lost in the vastness of the scenery as their footsteps in the sand."

The greatest advantages of walking to Thoreau's explorations are most evident in his land explorations, when his feet were planted on the solid ground of the Concord forest, fields, and hills. Thoreau was particularly attuned to the forest floor. He carefully studied the plants and animals that filled the forest. When walking in the woods,

Thoreau frequently rested; and he used his resting time, not to meditate idly, but to observe as this *Journal* (Princeton) entry notes: "He who traverses the woodland paths will have occasion to remember the small drooping bell-like flowers, and slender red stem of the dog's bane—which were the subject of his study while resting from his walk."

Thoreau's epigeal excursions frequently entailed hard work and considerable sweat. Just reaching the plants he wished to study, and traversing the terrain along the way, made the adventures challenging. Thoreau transformed the traditional view of the study of plants. In his day many held that botany was an activity primarily for ladies interested in "delicate colors and textures," but Thoreau established the study of plants as "a very rugged, masculine occupation" (Eifert).

Thoreau's neighbors might not have appreciated his study of wildflowers, but he earned their respect when he studied their trees. When his neighbors asked him why their hardwood lots, once cut down, often became pine woods and vice versa, he commenced his rigorous study of this phenomenon. To answer their question, Thoreau walked systematically through the Concord woods, collecting seeds of the various trees to study them, carefully examining the forest undergrowth, and digging up seedlings to examine factors like their root systems. He discovered that if a pine wood were cut, the young oaks in the subgrowth that had a deeper root system than the young pines would supplant them, while if an oak wood were cut, the more abundant seed of the pines was likely to produce a pine stand. The results of his study, published in his essay "The Succession of Forest Trees," furthered his contemporaries' knowledge of forest growth and maintenance, as did his later study of stump rings.

From the forest floor, Thoreau often traveled into

nearby mountains. His rock climbing put him in concrete contact with the raw, rugged side of nature's surface. We can read of one such excursion to Mount Monadnock that Thoreau recorded in his *Journal*. The rugged and varied features of the mountain's surface disoriented the walker and reminded him, as Cape Cod had before, of man's fragile and tentative position when placed in such a vast and overwhelming landscape: "We had thus made a pretty complete survey of the top of the mountain. It is a very unique walk, and would be almost equally interesting to take though it were not elevated above the surrounding valleys. It often reminded me of my walks on the beach, and suggested how much both depend for their sublimity on solitude and dreariness. In both cases we feel the presence of some vast, titanic power."

Although somewhat discomfited by the mountain's inhospitable surface, Thoreau found his attention directed toward the clouds, which offered him both entertainment and insight. Free to gaze at the clouds at will and to observe their patterns and movements, Thoreau recorded his reaction: "It was interesting to watch from that height the shadows of fair-weather clouds passing over the landscape. You could hardly distinguish them from the forests. . . . We do not commonly realize how constant and amusing a phenomenon this is in a summer day to one standing on a sufficiently elevated point. . . . It was pleasant enough to see one man's farm in the shadow of a cloud,—which perhaps he thought covered all the Northern States,—while his neighbor's farm was in sunshine."

Thoreau's sauntering explorations spanned all the surface features of the landscape, probing the phenomena of earth, sea, and sky. The contact of his feet or the reach of his senses put him in concrete touch with these surfaces, drawing him close to Nature, whose secrets he sought. Walking allowed him to examine thoroughly the phenomena of each landscape, filling his walks with discoveries and adventures.

One problem, however, that Thoreau faced in his exploration of the landscape was that the features of the land that he sought to explore and understand changed continually from moment to moment and from season to season. Nature was a chameleon in the hands of seasonal and climactic changes. What seemed true one day might appear different tomorrow or next month.

One important characteristic of Thoreau's walking experience—the direct result of his desire to know Nature in all of its moods—was its comprehensiveness. In an effort to study Nature in all her manifestations, Thoreau walked outdoors at all times in all seasons. He knew all too well the difference a change in season or climate could make: "It is a little affecting to walk over the hills now, looking at the reindeer lichens here and there amid the snow, and remember that ere long we shall find violets also in their midst. What an odds [difference] the season make!"

In "Country Life" Emerson exclaimed, "I think sometimes how many days could Methuselah go out and find something new!" According to Emerson, each month of the year and each season offers the explorer something new, something exciting. The transcendental saunterer explored each seasonal and daily manifestation of the landscape with an appropriate air of expectancy, as Thoreau made clear in his *Journal:* "Not only different objects are presented to our attention at different seasons of the year, but we are in a frame of body and of mind to appreciate different objects at different seasons. I see one thing when it is cold and another when it is warm."

Walking proved the best form of travel for the explorer since it allowed him to saunter at any time and under any circumstances. Bad weather and difficult terrain never deterred Thoreau from walking into Nature to study it. In fact, he often rambled forth under circumstances that kept most of his contemporaries at home.

Many of his spring and summer walks were intentionally taken during inclement weather. Thoreau believed that to explore the wilder side of Nature, one needed to take wilder walks. Walks during wild weather yielded discoveries that walks during fair weather would not make possible, a point made in an April *Journal* entry: "To see the larger and wilder birds, you must go forth in the great storms like this. At such times they frequent our neighborhood and trust themselves in our midst. A life of fair-weather walks might never show you the goose sailing on our waters, or the great heron feeding here. When the storm increases, then these great birds that carry the mail of the seasons lay to. To see wild life you must go forth at a wild season. When it rains and blows, keeping men indoors, then the lover of Nature must forth. Then returns Nature to her wild estate."

Thoreau believed in converting foul weather into an opportunity for further discovery. Walking provided him with the flexibility to adjust his exploration to the demands of the weather. During one spring walk he recorded: "Such a day as this, I resort where the partridges, etc., do—to the bare ground and the sheltered sides of woods and hills—and there explore the moist ground for the radical leaves of plants, while the storm blows overhead, and I forget how the time is passing. If the weather is thick and stormy enough, if there is a good chance to be cold and wet and uncomfortable, in other words to feel weather-beaten, you may consume the afternoon to advantage thus browsing along the edge of some near wood which would scarcely detain you at all in fair weather, and you will [be] as far away there as at the end of your longest fair-weather walk, and come home as if from an adventure. There is no better fence to put between you and the village than a storm into which the villagers do not venture out." Any unusual weather conditions attracted Thoreau to take a walk in hopes of discovering something new: "A great drought now for several weeks. . . . A good time to visit swamps and meadows."

In his rambles Thoreau often walked in the rain or overcast conditions and found such excursions rewarding: "They who do not walk in the woods in the rain never behold them in their freshest, most radiant and blooming beauty." In *A Week* Thoreau notes how walking allows the saunterer to seek shelter from a hard rain wherever he likes, and to explore his surroundings at his leisure: "When compelled by a shower to take shelter under a tree, we may improve that opportunity for a more minute inspection of some of Nature's works. I have stood under a tree in the woods half a day at a time, during a heavy rain in the summer, and yet employed myself happily and profitably there prying with microscopic eye into the crevices of the bark or the leaves or the fungi at my feet." Even cloudy days compelled Thoreau to refocus his exploration by altering his walking pattern: "When the air is thick and the sky overcast, we need not walk so far. We give our attention to nearer objects, being less distracted from them. I take occasion to explore some near wood which my walks commonly overshoot."

When winter came, Thoreau adapted his walks to the new conditions. In a December 1859 *Journal* entry, he recorded the import of his first winter walk for that year: "My first true winter walk is perhaps that which I take on the river, or where I cannot go in the summer. It is the walk peculiar to winter, and now first I take it. I see that the fox too has already taken the same walk before me, just along the edge of the button-bushes, where not even he can go in the summer. We both turn our steps hither at the same time."

Winter sauntering was particularly difficult, and Thoreau was fully aware of the diminishing returns involved in casting oneself into a cold, barren landscape in search of discoveries. Although he was often frustrated with winter walking, he held that the few trophies gleaned during a winter walk were equal in value to the numerous discoveries made during summer hiking. The more vigorous and difficult the walk, the more valued the discoveries, even if they were few in number, as this November 1857 *Journal* description indicates: "The prospect looks so barren, so many springs are frozen up, not a flower perchance and but few birds left, not a companion abroad in all these fields for me, I am slow to go forth. I seem to anticipate a fruitless walk. I think to myself hesitatingly, Shall I go there, or there, or there? and cannot make up my mind to any route, all seem so unpromising, mere surface walking and fronting the cold wind, so that I have to force myself to it often and at random. But then I am often unexpectedly compensated, and the thinnest yellow light of November is more warming and exhilarating than any wine they tell of; and then the mite which November contributes becomes equal in value to the bounty of July."

In *Walden* Thoreau describes his persistent efforts to flush discoveries from nature in the wintertime, frequently tramping "eight or ten miles through the deepest snow to keep an appointment with a beech tree, or a yellow-birch, or an old acquaintance among the pines." During harsh walking conditions he "rarely failed to find, even in mid-winter, some warm and springy swamp where the grass and the skunk-cabbage still put forth with perennial verdure, and some hardier bird occasionally awaited the return of spring."

Thoreau's snow walks opened up new vistas to his sauntering eye: "How new all things seem! Here is a broad, shallow pool in the fields, which yesterday was slosh, now converted into a soft, white, fleecy snow ice, like bread that has spewed out and baked outside the pan. It is like the beginning of the world. There is nothing hackneyed where a new snow can come and cover all the landscape." Each new snow transforms the landscape: "We discover a new world every time that we see the earth again after it has been covered for a season with snow."

Even more, however, than offering a new surface to view, snow and ice provided Thoreau with the opportunity to traverse the land in places where summer hiking would have been very difficult or impossible. Thoreau made this clear in "A Winter Walk," where he observed: "No domain of nature is quite closed to man at all times, and now we draw near to the empire of the fishes. Our feet glide swiftly over unfathomed depths, where in summer our line tempted the pout and perch, and where the stately pickerel lurked in the long corridors formed by the bulrushes. The deep, impenetrable marsh, where the heron waded and bittern squatted, is made pervious to our swift shoes, as if a thousand railroads had been made into it."

Snow cover allowed Thoreau to explore the movements of nature. He not only enjoyed tracking animals, but especially liked to recreate experience by interpreting the imprints he found in the snow. His inquisitive nature drove him to solve, in detective fashion, the snow puzzles that he encountered. His *Journal* records a number of such attempts to interpret snowy hieroglyphics. One entry begins with an account of his efforts to solve the mystery posed by fox and rabbit tracks: "In Hosmer's pitch pine wood just north of the bridge, I find myself on the track of a fox—as I take it—that has run about a great deal. Next I come to the tracks of rabbits, see where they have travelled back and forth, making a well-trodden path in the snow; and soon after I see where one has been killed and apparently devoured." A mysterious mark in the snow a few yards from the point where the rabbit was apparently killed led Thoreau to conclude that the fox had also flushed a partridge. Closer investigation helped him realize that an owl was the culprit, first killing the rabbit, and then, startled by the fox, carrying the rabbit to a safer place to enjoy his meal. Thoreau pieced the details together: "Now I understand how that furrow was made, the bird with the rabbit in its talons flying low there, and now I remember that at the first bloody spot I saw some of these quill-marks; and therefore it is certain that the bird had it there, and probably he killed it, and he, perhaps disturbed by the fox, carried it to the second place, and it is certain that he (probably disturbed by the fox again) carried it to the last place, making a furrow on the way. If it had not been for the snow on the ground I probably should not have noticed any signs that a rabbit had been killed. Or, if I had chanced to see the scattered fur, I should not have known what creature did it, or how recently."

Thoreau also noted deer-mice tracks in the snow, where the mice had "hopped over the soft snow last night, scarcely making any impression." Excited by the thrill of verifying the presence and activity of creatures normally unseen to man, Thoreau had concrete evidence of the mysterious life of the forest at night: "What if you could witness with owl's eyes the revelry of the wood mice some night, frisking about the wood like so many little kangaroos? Here is a palpable evidence that the woods are nightly thronged with little creatures which most have never seen,—populousness as commonly only the imagination dreams of." As Thoreau put it, "how much the snow reveals!" to the winter saunterer traversing the snowy landscape.

Human tracks in the snow symbolized for Thoreau the interconnectedness of man's experience—a reminder that men walk the same ground, even if their experiences are not always the same. These tracks pointed to walking as an important common denominator of human experience: "I cannot now walk without leaving a track behind me; that is one peculiarity of winter walking. Anybody may follow my trail. I have walked, perhaps, a particular wild path along some swampside all summer, and thought to myself, I am the only villager that ever comes here. But I go out shortly after the first snow has fallen, and lo, here is the track of a sportsman and his dog in my secluded path, and probably he preceded me in the summer as well. Yet my hour is not his, and I may never meet him!"

In an earlier *Journal* account recording a summer walk, Thoreau also focused on the bond between men which walking signifies: "I see the track of a bare human foot in the dusty road, the toes and muscles all faithfully imprinted. Such a sight is so rare that it affects me with surprise, as the footprint on the shore of Juan Fernandez did Crusoe. It is equally rare here. I am affected as if some Indian or South-Sea-Islander had been along, some man who had a foot. . . . It is pleasant as it is to see the tracks of cows and deer and birds. I am brought so much nearer to the tracker—when again I think of the sole of my own foot—than when I behold that of his shoe merely, or am introduced to him and converse with him in the usual way."

Thoreau's determination to know all the surface features of nature led him to more than just seasonal or climatic walking experiences. His natural inquisitiveness also drove him to night walking. He began hiking late at night during times when a full moon benefitted his vision. In his essay "Night and Moonlight" Thoreau acknowledged his commitment to nighttime exploring: "Chancing to take a memorable walk by moonlight some years ago, I resolved to take more such walks, and make acquaintance with another side of nature: I have done so." In this same essay Thoreau shared his enchantment with the novelty and diversity of nighttime sauntering: "I shall be a benefactor if I conquer some realms from the night, if I report to the gazettes anything transpiring about us at that season worthy of their attention,—if I can show men that there is some beauty awake while they are asleep,—if I add to the domains of poetry. Night is certainly more novel and less profane than day. I soon discovered that I was acquainted only with its complexion, and as for the moon, I had seen her only as it were through a crevice in a shutter, occasionally. Why not walk a little way in her light?"

Thoreau was particularly sensitive to the transformations moonlight and darkness worked on the landscape that he knew so well by daylight. Problems with depth perception made night walking challenging, and objects presented themselves more conspicuously at night, often assuming strange or foreboding shapes: "The potatoes stand up straight, the corn grows, the bushes loom, and, in a moonlight night, the shadows of rocks and trees and bushes and hills are more conspicuous than the objects themselves. The slightest inequalities in the ground are revealed by the shadows; what the feet find comparatively smooth appears rough and diversified to the eye. The smallest recesses in the rocks are dim and cavernous; the ferns in the wood appear to be of tropical size; the pools seen through the leaves become as full of light as the sky. . . . The woods are heavy and dark. Nature slumbers."

Whether walking during the day or night Thoreau traversed the same countryside, time and time again. He did not feel the compulsion to travel far and widely. He could explore whatever he needed too close to home and never fully exhaust the possibilities for discovery. Consequently, most of his walks were local, occurring within a ten-mile radius of his home. Thoreau viewed these walks as he did his own life—full of inexhaustible possibilities, and he was not bothered by the boundaries of his walking experience any more than he was by the mortal limits to his own existence. In "Walking" he notes how no matter how restricted the experience, new discoveries and experiences were still possible: "My vicinity affords many good walks; and though for so many years I have walked almost every day, and sometimes for several days together, I have not yet exhausted them. An absolutely new prospect is a great happiness, and I can still get this any afternoon. Two or three hours' walking will carry me to as strange a country as I expect ever to see. A single farmhouse which I had not seen before is sometimes as good as the dominions of the King of Dahomey. There is in fact a sort of harmony discoverable between the capabilities of the landscape within a circle of ten miles' radius, or the limits of an afternoon walk, and the threescore years and ten of human life. It will never become quite familiar to you."

Thoreau's walking experience, like his life, was quite parochial. At a time when his coutrymen traveled abroad or headed west to seek their discoveries, Thoreau remained in the Concord area, devoting the majority of his time to a study of nature. Thoreau's commitment to this small share of New England soil resulted in part from his own love for Concord, which was, according to Thoreau, the only place for a saunterer like himself to live. He counted it his fortune to have been placed in such a fertile environment: "I have never got over my surprise that I should have been born into the most estimable place in all the world, and in the very nick of time, too." No other place could have so adequately satisfied his quest to know nature and to know it thoroughly: "I cannot but regard it as a kindness in those who have the steering of me that, by the want of pecuniary wealth, I have been nailed down to this my native region so long and steadily, and made to study and love this spot of earth more and more. What would signify in comparison a thin and diffused love and knowledge of the whole earth instead, got by wandering?"

Walking so often within the well-established limits of the Concord area also affirmed for Thoreau his roots and his heritage. Concord was the city of his birth; its fields and forests connected to the memories of his childhood. Thoreau's local rambles not only pressed the mud and dirt of Concord into his boots, they also embedded in his inner consciousness a powerful sense of Concord itself. His constant saunterings around his home city so attached him to it, that he was never quite able to escape its influence on him, nor did he want to.

Thoreau's correspondence during the time when he stayed in Staten Island reveals his deep attachment to Concord. In May 1843 he wrote Mrs. Emerson: "I carry Concord ground in my boots and in my hat,—And am I not made of Concord dust? I cannot realize that it is the roar of the sea I hear now, and not the wind in Walden woods." In another May letter, this one to his mother, he confided: "All my inner man heretofore has been a Concord impression; and here come these Sandy Hook and Coney Island breakers to meet and modify the former; but it will be long before I can make nature look as innocently grand and inspiring as in Concord." In July he felt much the same way, expressing to Mr. and Mrs. Emerson that he continually found his thoughts turning to "those dear hills and that river which so fills up the world to its brim." He assured them that the things he remembered of Concord were "better than the environs of New York."

With the aid of Thoreau's active imagination, the boundaries of Concord spilled over into any place that he traveled to, causing him to see and feel the Concord environment regardless of his present setting. He could not neatly distinguish Concord from other places, as this August 1843 statement to his mother indicates: "Methinks I should be content to sit at the back-door in Concord, under the poplar-tree, henceforth forever. Not that I am homesick at all,—for places are strangely indifferent to me,—but Concord is still a cynosure to my eyes, and I find it hard to attach it, even in imagination, to the rest of the globe, and tell where the seam is." The Concord environment made Thoreau feel at home; it affected him like a familiar friend. He could not imagine walking or being anywhere else: "Think of the consummate folly of attempting to go away from here! When the constant endeavor should be to get nearer and nearer here. . . . Take the shortest way round and stay at home. A man dwells in his native valley like a corolla in its calyx, like an acorn in its cup. Here, of course, is all that you love, all that you expect, all that you are. Here is your bride elect, as close to you as she can be got. Here is all the best and all the worst you can imagine. What more do you want?"

Thoreau's saunters drew him close to the Concord environment—his "bride elect." But Thoreau confined most of his walks to the Concord area for other reasons as well. He disdained superficial enterprises of any kind, and exploring was no exception. He viewed the typical traveler's experience as highly superficial; only careful sauntering could make possible a thorough acquaintance with the surface features of the landscape. Thoreau expressed this point of view in his *Journal* when he described gazing at the nearby town of Sudbury and conjecturing: "I see its meeting-houses and its common, and its fields lie but little beyond my ordinary walk, but I never played on its common nor read the epitaphs in its graveyard, and many strangers to me dwell there. . . . How circumscribed are our walks, after all! With the utmost industry we cannot expect to know well an area more than six miles square, and yet we pretend to be travellers, to be acquainted with Siberia and Africa!"

Thoreau felt that the successful saunterer concentrated

his explorations at home and not abroad. He notes that "there would be this advantage in travelling in your own country, even in your own neighborhood, that you would be so thoroughly prepared to understand what you saw you would make fewer travellers' mistakes." Traveling at home gives the saunterer the advantage of always adding to the knowledge he already possesses of the local environment; traveling away from home only contributes to the explorer's ignorance of a new and unfamiliar territory: "How often it happens that the traveller's principal distinction is that he is one who knows less about a country than a native! Now if he should begin with all the knowledge of a native, and add thereto the knowledge of a traveller, both natives and foreigners would be obliged to read his book; and the world would be absolutely benefited. It takes a man of genius to travel in his own country, in his native village; to make any progress between his door and his gate." The explorer who saunters at home instead of abroad allows himself all the advantages that a thorough examination of the landscape provides.

Thoreau was not easily enticed away from his native fields. He knew that the saunterer who remained home was somehow freer and better able to express himself than the one who traveled afar, and he recognized that there is "nothing like one's native fields and lakes." Walking daily in the same area allowed Thoreau to know his native soil and to know himself better: "A man is worth most to himself and to others, whether as an observer, or poet, or neighbor, or friend, where he is most himself, most contented and at home. There his life is the most intense and he loses the fewest moments. Familiar and surrounding objects are the best symbols and illustrations of his life. . . . The man who is often thinking that it is better to be somewhere else than where he is excommunicates himself. If a man is rich and strong anywhere, it must be on his native soil. Here I have been these forty years learning the language of these fields that I may better express myself."

Thoreau could explore all that he needed to within a short distance of his house: "I seem to have reached a new world, so wild a place that the very huckleberries grew hairy and were inedible. . . . What's the need of visiting far-off mountains and bogs, if a half-hour's walk will carry me into such wildness and novelty? . . . It is in vain to dream of a wildness distant from ourselves. There is none such. It is the bog in our brain and bowels, the primitive vigor of Nature in us, that inspires that dream. I shall never find in the wilds of Labrador any greater wildness than in some recess in Concord, i. e. than I import into it."

Such claims for his local town were typical for Thoreau. R. W. Emerson comments on Thoreau's penchant to extol "his own town and neighborhood as the most favored center for natural observation" ("Thoreau"). Although Thoreau followed the trail of other explorers during his trips to Cape Cod, Maine, and elsewhere, in Concord he was the adventurer finding there what others sought in other places.

One benefit of Thoreau's resolve to do his walking at home was that his walks placed his life in perspective and reinforced his own centrality in the miniature universe he explored on a daily basis. It is the nature of walking to do this—to place things in perspective and reduce them to a smaller, more manageable scale.

In the Concord area Thoreau viewed himself as living in a microcosm. He was the center of the circle, and his walks provided the radius to link him with his microcosm's outer limits. Thus wherever he walked, whatever the environment, the heart of the microcosm was where he was, radiating out from his presence. Such was the case at Walden, where he noted: "But for the most part it is as solitary where I live as on the prairies. It is as much Asia or Africa as New England. I have, as it were, my own sun and moon and stars, and a little world all to myself."

Thoreau's local walks helped him explore his own little world, and since they took place within reach of Concord, Concord remained for him a symbol of his microcosm. Frederick Garber provides a helpful perspective of the interdependent relationship between Thoreau's self and Concord as the focuses for his microcosm: "It was Thoreau's habit to localize whatever consciousness could absorb, and since the most local was the selfhood within him, all alien materials ultimately ended up there. Thoreau's construction of experience . . . placed his consciousness at the center of a concentric series of enclosures or clearings. Outside the self was Concord, and outside that was the wild and, finally, the world. Everything beyond Concord eventually had reference to the town."

Converting an area like Concord into a microcosm by studying it in detail is perfectly suited to the walker. "The walker does not need a large territory," notes Burroughs, who adds: "When you get into a railway car you want a continent, the man in his carriage requires a township; but a walker like Thoreau finds as much and more along the shores of Walden Pond. The former, as it were, has merely time to glance at the headings of the chapters, while the latter need not miss a line, and Thoreau reads between the lines" (The Exhilarations of the Road"). Walking, then, equipped Thoreau to convert the Concord countryside into a transcendental microcosm that responded to his deliberate and thorough sauntering explorations with insights into the universal.

Emerson and Thoreau held similar views about the concept of a microcosm. In *Nature* Emerson noted the relationship of the part to the whole, the microcosm to the macrocosm: "A leaf, a drop, a crystal, a moment of time, is related to the whole, and partakes of the perfection of the whole. Each particle is a microcosm, and faithfully renders the likeness of the world." In his poem "Each and All" he reaffirmed the important relationship between the part and the whole: "All are needed by each one; / Nothing is fair or good alone." This poem demonstrates how all parts of the landscape contribute to the whole, and the viewer's joy is derived from the sense of the whole which the parts provide: "Beauty through my senses stole; / I yielded myself to the perfect whole."

While on his walks, Thoreau applied this same viewpoint to his discoveries. R. W. Emerson claimed of Thoreau, "I know not any genius who so swiftly inferred universal law from the single fact" ("Thoreau"). According to Emerson, for Thoreau "there was no such thing as size." Details of the landscape often suggested themselves to larger truths or perspectives. "The pond was a small ocean; the Atlantic, a large Walden Pond." Everywhere he walked, "he referred every minute fact to cosmical laws" ("Thoreau").

James Joyce had his Dublin, William Faulkner his Yoknapatawpha County, and Henry Thoreau his Concord. Each of these authors relied on a geographical base to provide the microcosm from which the universal nature of their works could be perceived. But more than a literary focal point, Concord provided Thoreau with a place to survey the landscape and learn firsthand the universal significance of the particulars he discovered. As literary characters, Leopold Bloom and Stephen Dedalus walked through Dublin, their particular experiences informing the reader of the universals affecting Ireland and the human condition. But Henry Thoreau needed no literary character to do the same for him. He walked through Concord himself, learning and then sharing with the reader the universal signficance of his experiences.

As has been pointed out, the walker's physical self provided one center, a mobile one, from which to interpret discoveries made in the microcosm, and Concord provided a geographical center for such discoveries. But a third factor, the saunterer's imaginative self, broadened the base of the walker's viewpoint. Because of his vast reading and his active imagination, Thoreau was able to project himself into places and situations well removed from his present location. This allowed him to draw analogies between his local discoveries and other places, and it enabled him to better connect the particulars of his Concord experience with the whole of whatever larger scene he could visualize. Thus imaginative sauntering combined with literal walking to produce discoveries with both local and universal significance.

Frederick Garber comments on Thoreau's ability to extend his reach beyond Concord by tapping his imagination. According to Garber, Thoreau "postulated a map for his imagination" out of his immediate surroundings and "the geography of the North American continent." He treated the "North American wilderness" as though it "began just at the edge of the boundaries of Concord and extended out from there in reaches which seemed infinite because they encompassed a major continent." Thoreau's penchant to imaginatively project himself beyond his immediate locale is evident in *Walden,* where he writes: "Though the view from my door was still more contracted, I did not feel crowded or confined in the least. There was pasture enough for my imagination. The low shrub-oak plateau to which the opposite shore arose, stretched away toward the prairies of the West and the steppes of Tartary, affording ample room for all the roving families of men. . . . Both place and time were changed, and I dwelt nearer to those parts of the universe and to those eras in history which had most attracted me. Where I lived was as far off as many a region viewed nightly by astronomers."

Thoreau's reading provided him with the material that his imagination could use to engage in mental sauntering away from Concord. John Christie, whose book *Thoreau as World Traveler* (1965) studies the major influence that travel reading had on Thoreau, describes a particular instance illustrating how easily Thoreau's reading affected his walking experience: "So closely did Thoreau identity himself with the travelers on these routes [arctic explorations] that he found it difficult to leave their company. He did much of his reading about the Arctic in the winter months (as, interestingly enough, he did much of his vicarious tropical traveling in the summer), when the world outside the kitchen window lent itself with particular congeniality to his imaginings. When he finally put down his book to pursue his daily outdoor activities, so close to the surface lay the experiences of his reading that like the icebergs on his northern routes they were constantly looming through the Concord landscape, polar 'refractions' against a New England background."

Thoreau walked through Concord to discover its every detail, but he read about foreign places to learn about the world outside of Concord and to connect that world with Concord. Thoreau's walks often functioned at two levels. There was the literal physical level of the walk itself, which placed the walker in the local environment; and there was the psychological level of imaginative sauntering, by which the walker applied his travel reading to the literal walking experience. The walker's physical and mental sauntering produced a hybrid experience that related the local, particular adventure with a more distant or universal focus.

The effect of this bi-level perspective is evident in his *Journal*, where Thoreau frequently compares the local landscape and those discoveries made while he walked in the Concord countryside with foreign places and discoveries made abroad. In many *Journal* entries such comparisons appear when he extols the higher value of a local discovery over that of the foreign one. In one November entry Thoreau argues: "Famous fruits imported from the tropics and sold in our markets—as oranges, lemons, pineapples, and bananas—do not concern me so much as many an unnoticed wild berry whose beauty annually lends a new charm to some wild walk, or which I have found to be palatable to an outdoor taste. . . . It is not the foreignness or size or nutritive qualities of a fruit that determine its absolute value."

In a November 1858 *Journal* entry Thoreau describes his view of a local bay while he was walking near Walden: "Some are hastening to Europe and some to the West Indies, but here is a bay never steered for. These nameless bays where the *Times* and *Tribune* have no correspondent are the true bays of All Saints for me." A similar sentiment is recorded in other *Journal* accounts of Thoreau's walks. In one description he recounts picking up a beautiful lily and observing that "men will travel to the Nile to see the lotus flower, who have never seen in their glory the lotuses of their native streams." In a different entry he exonerates local moonlight walks by stating that there is "no need to climb the Andes or Himalayas, for brows of lowest hills are highest mountain-tops in cool moonlight nights."

Several *Journal* entries evoke more favorable references to the foreign places Thoreau had read about. Even something as unromantic as cow droppings could draw a memory from Thoreau's reading. During one walk Thoreau reflected: "I notice some old cow-droppings in a pasture, which are decidedly pink. Even these trivial objects awaken agreeable associations in my mind, connected not only with my own actual rambles but with what I have read of the prairies and pampa and Eastern land of grass, the great pastures of the world." When hiking in a swamp, Thoreau's spotting of a hummingbird made him think that he "was in the tropics,—in Demerara or Maracaibo."

There was much in the Concord environment that reminded Thoreau of faraway places. Everywhere he walked he was aware of both his local region and those regions beyond it. Thus he could exclaim about the invigorating nature of a Concord spring: "A certain dormant life awakes in me, and I begin to love nature again. Here is my Italy, my heaven, my New England." Wherever he went his travel reading expanded the world of his walks, reaching out to places where Thoreau would never walk nor visit. While on one sauntering adventure, Thoreau observed: "Our humble scenery appears on a grand scale. I see the fair forms of mighty pines standing along a mountain ridge above the clouds and overlooking from a vast distance our low valley. . . . The appearance of those fine-edged pines, a narrow strip of a mountain ridge half a mile in length, is stupendous and imposing. It is as if we lived in a valley amid the Himmalaya Mountains, a vale of Cashmere."

There were times, of course, when Thoreau literally and not merely imaginatively left the Concord area. He was averse to any type of rut or custom, and so he periodically broke his local walking pattern for a change of scenery and experience. According to Thoreau, these journeys served the purpose of giving his intellect "an airing."

A few of these trips outside the Concord area involved walks to nearby towns or mountains. These modest excursions were usually inspired by Thoreau's curiosity about these places. In his *Journal* he briefly recalls one such experience: "We journeyed into the foreign land of Sudbury to see how the Sudbury men—the Hayneses, and the Puffers, and the Brighams—live. We traversed their pastures and their wood-lots, and were home again at night." Such trips were informing, but not necessarily inspiring.

Thoreau, however, was driven well beyond places like Sudbury, traveling to Maine, Canada, Cape Cod, Minnesota, and other distant places. It was his nature that as soon as he had explored an area and become familiar with it, he felt the impulse to extend his exploration, either by studying the same area more intensely or by expanding the range of his explorations. In his *Journal* (Princeton) he notes: "These continents and hemispheres are the prey of a speedy familiarity—but always an unexplored and infinite region makes off on every side from my mind—as near as Cathay, and as far too. I can make no high way or beaten track into it, but immediately the grass springs up in the path."

Thoreau took these lengthy journeys to study different landscapes, to view firsthand nature's varied surfaces. According to Richard Schneider, Thoreau challenged his neighbors to do the same, urging them to "explore the infinitely advancing frontiers of nature and of the human mind." Once his townsmen, like himself, had explored the local landscape, other places would beckon.

Walking played an important role in most of these longer excursions, though it was seldom as satisfying nor as meaningful as was his local walking experience. In "A Yankee in Canada" he reveals the unfulfilled impulse to walk that he experienced during his trip to Canada: "I fear that I have not got much to say about Canada, not having seen much; what I got by going to Canada was a cold. . . . I wished only to be set down in Canada, and take one honest walk there as I might in Concord woods of an afternoon." Thoreau discovered during his Canadian excursion that walking outside of Concord was generally a disappointing experience. His one major walk while in Canada lacked the intensity and insight that characterized his daily saunterings in Concord.

Thoreau's trips to Cape Cod were almost exclusively foot journeys—"I travelled the length of Cape Cod on foot," and he found them considerably more rewarding than his Canada trip. His *Journal* account of one of these trips reveals his enthusiasm for the walking experience: "Though we walked all day, it seemed the days were not long enough to get tired in." On the Cape, Thoreau was able to do what had been denied him in Canada—to get away from civilization and walk in nature, exploring its unadulterated features.

One interesting difference between Thoreau's walking adventures while exploring away from Concord and his sauntering experiences in Concord is the fact that when away from Concord, he sought the novel and the un-usual. In his *Journal* he comments: "The discoveries which we make abroad are special and particular; those which we make at home are general and significant. The further off, the nearer the surface. The nearer home, the deeper." In *Cape Cod* he confesses that "we did not care to see those features of the Cape in which it is inferior or merely equal to the mainland, but only those in which it is peculiar or superior."

Because he sought novelty, Thoreau found it particu-larly rejuvenating to make sauntering discoveries abroad as this *Journal* entry indicates: "Would it not be worth the while to discover Nature in Milton [Milton, Massa-chusetts]? Be native to the universe. I, too, love Concord best, but I am glad when I discover, in oceans and wilder-nesses far away, the materials out of which a million Con-cords can be made,—indeed, unless I discover them, I am lost myself,—that there too I am at home." When he returned from his Maine trip with Edward Hoar, he noted in a letter that "the world appears in some respects a little larger, and not, as usual, smaller and shallower, for having extended our range." His contact with the American Indian excited him most about this excursion— "he is so much the more divine; and anything that fairly excites our admiration expands us." Much of this admiration had stemmed from Thoreau's portages with his Indian guide over difficult terrain. His shared walking experience with the Indian was something that could not be done in Concord and thus had made the Maine trip particularly rewarding.

Sauntering discoveries made abroad could be profitable in yet another way. When Thoreau came across a new phenomenon away from Concord, he studied it closely; and once familiar with it, he then sought it in Concord. Some of the walking discoveries that he made in Concord were the direct result of previous discoveries abroad: "Thus I have within a week found in Concord two of the new plants I found up-country. Such is the advantage of going abroad,—to enable [you] to detect your own plants. I detected them first abroad, because there I was looking for the strange." In *Huckleberries* Thoreau observes, "I have added a few to my number of edible berries, by walking behind an Indian in Maine, and observing that he ate some which I never thought of tasting before."

Most aspects of his walking explorations remained the same for Thoreau, whether he walked abroad or walked locally. When walking abroad, he applied his travel reading to his foreign saunterings the same as he did when walking in Concord. We read in *Cape Cod* how Thoreau and his companion, protected under their umbrellas, traversed a sandy plain in a driving rainstorm, reading a travel book and imagining themselves transported to "such a moor as that on which somebody perished in the snow, as is related in the 'Lights and Shadows of Scottish Life.'" When plodding through a different part of the

Cape, he observed the "very strange scenery" of the surrounding landscape and conjectured, "You would think you might be in Labrador, or some other place you have imagined."

Thoreau practiced the concept of the microcosm wherever he traveled. His walks abroad reinforced for him that a man was the center of his own universe wherever he went, a notion he espoused in *A Week:* "It is an important epoch when a man who has always lived on the east side of a mountain, and seen it in the west, travels round and sees it in the east. Yet the universe is a sphere whose center is wherever there is intelligence. The sun is not so central as a man." Earlier in *A Week* Thoreau had described passing by a wooded island that sparked this observation: "An island always pleases by imagination, even the smallest, as a small continent and integral portion of the globe. I have a fancy for building my hut on one." Here is evidence of Thoreau's ability to take any feature of the landscape and convert it into a microcosm, a process he often employed during his saunterings. Even then, the walker himself remained the center of the microcosm, with the particular focal point of the landscape serving as a connector with the rest of the world. Wherever he traveled, Thoreau was himself the center of a microcosm, and he could project himself from that center to any point of the compass on the map of his imagination.

As has been shown, whether sauntering locally or abroad, Thoreau used walking as a medium to establish contact with and study the surfaces of nature. His feet carried him over every kind of terrain in every kind of weather and circumstance. His exploration was thorough, and, because of his careful mental and physical preparation, his walks yielded important discoveries that are carefully recorded in his *Journal* and his other writings. Walking helped Thoreau experience particular satisfaction in discovering the common when rambling locally or the uncommon when traveling abroad, and it proved the best travel form for aiding him in his quest to explore nature's surface as thoroughly as possible and to detect the universal significance of the particular phenomena that he studied. Physical and imaginative sauntering allowed Thoreau to create a portable, personal microcosm that expanded or contracted according to the walking environment and the walker's imagination, and which always kept the walker at the center of his personal universe, helping him to discover the physical landscape around him while relating it to those places that he had read about. In these various ways walking aided Thoreau's quest to explore thoroughly all the surface features of nature.

3

THE WORLD WITHIN

In *Walden* Thoreau resolved to "live deep and suck out all the marrow of life, to live so sturdily and Spartanlike as to put to rout all that was not life, to cut a broad swath and shave close, to drive life into a corner, and reduce it to its lowest terms." Like a bear clawing the bark from a log to reach the honey inside, Thoreau probed beneath nature's surface features seeking self-revelations. His walks tuned him to the world within himself.

The real focus of Thoreau's saunters was the experience of the walk—how it touched his inner landscape. In his *Journal* he commented that he was not "interested in mere phenomena, though it were the explosion of a planet, only as it may have lain in the experience of a human being." Thoreau thought it important to experience nature and not just to observe it: "A man has not seen a thing who has not felt it." When he sauntered into nature, his goal was not merely to observe surface phenomena, but to convert his observations into "such inward experience as will make nature significant."

The two most critical factors in determining the quality and nature of the walker's experiences are his attitude and the surrounding environment. The walker's attitude, in particular, significantly affects his experiences while he saunters. Thoreau advocated an open attitude. He allowed nature's influences free play, approaching his walks without preconceptions or prejudices that might interfere with the personal benefits from nature which he sought: "Nature is reported not by him who goes forth consciously as an observer, but in the fullness of life. To such a one she rushes to make her report. To the full heart she is all but a figure of speech." Understanding phenomena was not as important as experiencing and appreciating them, outcomes that were possible if the walker held the right attitude: "We shall see but little way if we require to understand what we see. How few things can a man measure with the tape of his understanding! How many greater things might he be seeing in the meanwhile!" Thoreau argues that the explorer should "take an original and unprejudiced view of Nature, letting her make what impression she will on you."

Thoreau was as free to saunter as he was to think; he could think and walk in any fashion he pleased, and he enjoyed a form of sauntering that left him open to the experiences which nature could stimulate: "You must walk sometimes perfectly free, not prying nor inquisitive, not bent upon seeing things. Throw away a whole day for a single expansion, a single inspiration of air."

Such free sauntering was advocated by Burroughs, who claimed that "success in walking is not to let your right foot know what your left foot doeth. Your heart must furnish such music that in keeping time to it your feet will carry you around the globe without knowing it." Annie Dillard claims that such walking involves a form of "letting go." The yielding of the saunterer's mental control to the influence of nature results in highly stimulating experiences. In *Pilgrim at Tinker Creek* she describes walking by a creek and giving herself to the magic of the moment as she observes minnows streaking through the water. The resulting experience is very Thoreauvian: "So I blurred my eyes and gazed towards the brim of my hat and saw a new world. I saw the pale white circles roll up, roll up, like the world's turning, mute and perfect, and I

73

saw linear flashes, gleaming silver, like stars being born at random down a rolling scroll of time. Something broke and something opened. I filled up like a new wineskin. I breathed an air like light; I saw a light like water. I was the lip of a fountain the creek filled forever; I was ether, the leaf in the zephyr; I was flesh-flake, feather, bone. When I see this way I see truly. As Thoreau says, I return to my senses."

An open attitude was especially important for Thoreau when his walks seemed profitless and he was tempted to terminate them. At times he found it best to extend his walks when he felt them a failure because he learned that his disarmed mood under such circumstances often made him more receptive to nature's influences: "When you think your walk is profitless and a failure, and you can hardly persuade yourself not to return, it is on the point of being a success, for then you are in that subdued and knocking mood to which Nature never fails to open." When describing one walk in his *Journal*, Thoreau reveals the important relationship between the walker's attitude and the fruitfulness of a walk: "This seems the true hour to be abroad sauntering far from home. Your thoughts being already turned toward home, your walk in one sense ended, you are in that favorable frame of mind described by DeQuicey, open to great impressions, and you see those rare sights with the unconscious side of the eye, which you could not see by a direct gaze before. Then the dews begin to descend in your mind, and its atmosphere is strained of all impurities; and home is farther away than ever. Here is home; the beauty of the world impresses you. There is a coolness in your mind as in a well. Life is too grand for supper."

Thoreau discovered that being lost and disoriented could, if viewed correctly, lead to rewarding experiences and insights. In his *Journal* he notes that "it is a surprising and memorable and, I may add, valuable experience to be lost in the woods, especially at night." He adds that "not till we are completely lost or turned round,—for a man needs only to be turned round once with his eyes shut in this world to be lost,—do we appreciate the vastness and strangeness of nature." Feeling lost disarms the walker's conscious expectation and renders him more open to the influences of the environment around him: "In fact, not till we are lost do we begin to realize where we are, and the infinite extent of our relations."

According to Thoreau, the walker's experience is enriched when he yields himself to a subliminal level of consciousness, freeing himself from external controls. Thoreau comments on this in *Walden,* where he describes walking at night in an absent-minded state: "Sometimes, after coming home thus late in a dark and muggy night, when my feet felt the path which my eyes could not see, dreaming and absent-minded all the way, until I was aroused by having to raise my hand to lift the latch, I have thought that perhaps my body would find its way home if its master should forsake it, as the hand finds its way to the mouth without assistance." He notes that during such walks the walker is guided "unconsciously" on his course until, at times, he truly becomes lost, resulting in a new discovery of himself and his relation to the world. According to this perspective, the walker really cannot be lost, provided he has followed the leadings of his inner genius. If the walker stays open to the influences around him—his experience will be profitable and his walk worthwhile, regardless of the conditions of the walk: "While each travels his own way through the wood with serene and inexpressible joy, though it be on his hands and knees over the rocks and fallen trees, he cannot but be on the right way; there is no wrong way to him. I have found myself as well off when I have fallen into a quagmire, as in an armchair in the most hospitable house. The prospect was pretty much the same. Without anxiety let us wander on, admiring whatever beauty the woods exhibit."

Along with the saunterer's attitude, the walker's immediate environment also affects the quality and nature of his inner experience. Thoreau was fully aware of the influence of the environment on his moods and thoughts. Channing, noting this, proclaims: "How [Thoreau] was affected by the seasons, who walked with them as a familiar friend! thinking thus aloud the thoughts which they brought; associations in linked sweetness long drawn out. . . ." In his *Journal* Thoreau observes that "in keeping a journal of one's walks and thoughts it seems to be worth the while to record those phenomena which are most interesting to us at the time. Such is the weather. It makes a material difference whether it is foul or fair, affecting surely our mood and thoughts." He notes: "In a journal it is important in a few words to describe the weather, or character of the day, as it affects our feelings," and then adds: "These regular phenomena of the seasons get at last to be—they were at first, of course—simply and plainly phenomena or phases of my life. The seasons and all their changes are in me."

When Thoreau walked in all seasons and environments, he often found his internal world corresponding to the external one: "The temperature of the air and the clearness or serenity of the sky are indispensable to a knowledge of a day, so entirely do we sympathize with the moods of nature."

But Thoreau did not find himself at the mercy of the environment every time he went for a walk. He used internal regulators to control his response to the environment and to help him experience nature in the most profitable way. In "A Winter Walk" he describes how "we step hastily along through the powdery snow, warmed by an inward heat, enjoying an Indian summer still, in the increased glow of thought and feeling." His ability to control his inner landscape when the external landscape threatened it is evident in this observation: "A healthy man, indeed, is the complement of the seasons, and in winter, summer is in his heart. There is the south. Thither have all birds and insects migrated, and around the warm springs in his breast are gathered the robin and the lark."

A passage in *A Week* also reveals the frequent contrast Thoreau experienced between the external and internal environment. When describing a very wet walk, Thoreau noted, "We managed to keep our thoughts dry, however, and only our clothes were wet."

Thoreau seemed to possess an intuitive sense of when it was best to control his inner landscape and when it was best to yield himself subconsciously to the influences of nature. One *Journal* description of a walk he took reveals this tension between the inner and outer landscapes and his response to it: "The mind is subject to moods, as the shadows of clouds pass over the earth. Pay not much heed to them. Let not the traveller stop for them. They consist with the fairest weather. By the mood of my mind, I suddenly felt dissuaded from continuing my walk, but I observed at the same instant that the shadow of a cloud was passing over [the] spot on which I stood, though it was of small extent, which, if it had no connection with my mood, at any rate suggested how transient and little to be regarded that mood was. I kept on, and in a moment the sun shone on my walk within and without."

Whether he exercised conscious control over the landscape or whether he yielded his control to the influence of the environment, when Thoreau walked in the Concord countryside from season to season he found himself subject to the influences of the weather. Each season brought him not only exciting discoveries of the external surface, but revelations and experiences that transformed his inner landscape.

Winter, more than any other season, affected Thoreau's thoughts and moods. In *Cape Cod* Thoreau notes how "an outward cold and dreariness, which make it necessary to seek shelter at night, lend a spirit of adventure to a walk." In his *Journal* Thoreau reveals how more than just the cold made a winter walk rewarding. The slant of the light evoked a special set of feelings: "Few things are more exhilarating . . . than to walk over bare pastures and see the abundant sheeny light like a universal halo, reflected from the russet and bleached earth." Such a light is "exceedingly warming to the spirits and imagination. This gives a character of snug warmth and cheerfulness to the swamp." The combination of the sunlight with melting snow particularly thrilled Thoreau: "How different the sunlight over thawing snow from the same over dry, frozen snow! The former excites me strangely, and I experience a springlike melting in my thoughts."

Nearly any phenomena that contrasted with the bleak winter landscape rejuvenated Thoreau's spirits and affected the quality of his thoughts and feelings. Springlike weather in January inspired this *Journal* note: "After December all weather that is not wintry is springlike. How changed are our feelings and thoughts by this more genial sky!" Hearing the cheering note of a chickadee break the icy, winter silence restored Thoreau's spirits: "All that is evergreen in me revived at once."

Even when uninterrupted by milder weather or the songs of birds, winter walking offered Thoreau special kinds of experiences. "I do not know of any more exhilarating walking," Thoreau said of ice walking. Thoreau viewed ice walking as inverted sauntering—that is, like sky walking: "The ice is a solid crystalline sky under our feet." He was fascinated by the reflections of the sky on the ice, and felt that the ice and sky sympathized with each other as their two surfaces met in winter time. Walking on such a surface "purified" and "translated" the saunterer. Walking on snow produced its own special effects: "So much higher do we carry our heads in winter. What a great odds such a little difference makes! When the snow raises us one foot higher than we have been accustomed to walk, we are surprised at our elevation! So we soar."

Winter sauntering did not always elicit positive feelings and experiences. Walking in a barren landscape could create, even for an individualist like Thoreau, an unwelcome sense of loneliness: "My walk is the more lonely when I perceive that there are no ants now upon their hillocks in field or wood. These are deserted mounds." The fierce New England wind could not only make him feel cold but "world-ridden" as well.

But no matter how he felt, Thoreau found winter more conducive to thinking than the other seasons: "The alert and energetic man leads a more intellectual life in winter than in summer. In summer the animal and vegetable in him are perfected as in a torrid zone; he lives in his senses mainly. In winter cold reason and not warm passion has her sway; he lives in thought and reflection; he lives a more spiritual, a less sensual, life."

Walking in other seasons affected Thoreau in similar ways, altering his inner landscape according to the external conditions that he faced. Warm spring air could stimulate "a revolution in our feelings," causing a "change mainly in us. We feel as if we had obtained a new lease on life." Warm summer air brings moisture, and rainy weather, like winter conditions, proved conducive to Thoreau's ability to think while he sauntered: "A rainy day is to the walker in solitude and retirement like the night. Few travellers are about, and they half hidden under umbrellas and confined to the highways. One's thoughts run in a different channel from usual." Thoreau records in his *Journal* that "rain is good for thought," and he observes: "I find it good to be out this still, dark, mizzling afternoon; my walk or voyage is more suggestive and profitable than in bright weather. The view is contracted by the misty rain, the water is perfectly smooth, and the stillness is favorable to reflection. I am more open to impressions, more sensitive (not calloused or indurated by sun and wind), as if in a chamber still. My thoughts are concentrated; I am all compact. Solitude is real, too, for the weather keeps other men at home. This mist is like a roof and walls over and around, and I walk with a domestic feeling."

In the fall the brisk air sparked Thoreau's internal saunterings: "I feel a cool vein in the breeze, which braces my thought."

Clear air spawned clear thoughts: "Methinks the reflections are never purer and more distinct than now at the season of the fall of the leaf, just before the cool twilight has come, when the air has a finer grain."

The time of day as well as the particular season affected the quality of Thoreau's experience. He discovered that walking before the heat of the day set in created "a feeling of vigor." Morning walking triggered a special air of expectancy, especially in spring: "As soon as those spring mornings arrive in which the birds sing, I am sure to be an early riser. I am waked by my genius. I wake to inaudible melodies and am surprised to find myself expecting the dawn in so serene and joyful and expectant a mood. I have an appointment with spring. She comes to the window to wake me, and I go forth an hour or two earlier than usual."

Daytime sauntering, however, often seemed more "trivial" to Thoreau than nighttime hiking did. As noted previously, Thoreau went on many evening walks, and during these walks, he not only saw natural phenomena from a different perspective, he also gained important insights into himself.

What made nighttime sauntering rewarding was the peace of mind and the intellectual awareness which it brought to the rambler. Thoreau comments in his *Journal* that walking at night plunges the hiker into a dream-like world which lulls his mental faculties into a very pleasant, subconscious state, one superior to the world-laden condition of the daytime traveller: "That kind of life which, sleeping, we dream that we live awake, in our walks by night, we, waking, live, while our daily life appears as a dream."

In his essay "Night and Moonlight" Thoreau has much to say regarding the internal benefits of nighttime sauntering. He comments on the effect night has on the saunterer's mental explorations—"As the shades begin to gather around us, our primeval instincts are aroused, and we steal forth from our lairs, like the inhabitants of the jungle, in search of those silent and brooding thoughts which are the natural prey of the intellect." The special effects of nighttime walking on his own spirit was something Thoreau could not pass by: "There are nights in this climate of such serene and majestic beauty, so medicinal and fertilizing to the spirit, that methinks a sensitive nature would not devote them to oblivion, and perhaps there is no man but would be better and wiser for spending them out-of-doors, though he should sleep all the next day to pay for it."

Walking in moonlight especially affects the saunterer. According to Thoreau, "No thinker can afford to overlook the influence of the moon any more than the astronomer can." He compares the moon's influence on the mind to its influence on the tides: "Is not the poet who walks by night conscious of a tide in his thought which is to be referred to lunar influence, in which the ocean within him overflows its shores and bathes the dry land?"

Thoreau carefully recorded in his *Journal* the effects of moonlight sauntering: "As the twilight deepens and the moonlight is more and more bright, I begin to distinguish myself, who I am and where; as my walls contract, I become more collected and composed, and sensible of my own existence, as when a lamp is brought into a dark apartment and I see who the company are. With the coolness and the mild silvery light, I recover some sanity, my thoughts are more distinct, moderated, and tempered. . . . I am sobered by the moonlight. I bethink myself. It is like a cup of cold water to a thirsty man. The moonlight is more favorable to meditation than sunlight." At night, when the moon worked its magic, Thoreau frequently found the quality of his inner experience deeply affected, as though the moonbeams could penetrate his exterior and reach his heart.

Whether Thoreau hiked at night or during the day, no matter what the season, every feature of the landscape and environment interacted with him to affect the quality of his experience. Thus he found himself intimidated by the openness of the Cape Cod road that he traveled during his trip to the Cape. As he describes in *Cape Cod*, an open landscape was not hospitable to someone from the New England woods: "We shuddered at the thought of living there and taking our afternoon walks over those barren swells, where we could overlook every step of our walk before taking it, and would have to pray for a fog or snow-storm to conceal our destiny. The walker there must soon eat his heart."

Even the quality of the air affected Thoreau, as his *Journal* reveals: "The influences which make for one walk more than another, and one day more than another, are much more ethereal than terrestrial. It is the quality of the air much more than the quality of the ground that concerns the walker,—cheers or depresses him. What he may find in the air, not what he may find on the ground."

His *Journal* record of his walks contains a number of references to the influence of the air on the saunterer. During one walk he noted that the "greater freshness and purity of the air" had the effect of rejuvenating "the spirits" of the walker. After a March walk, he recorded: "Though cloudy, the air excites me. Yesterday all was tight as a stricture on my breast; to-day all is loosened. . . . The sides of bushy hills where the snow is melted look, through this air, as if I were under the influence of some intoxicating liquor." Not just the quality of the air, but the wind itself, affects the walker's mood: "The thermometer does not give account of the wind, but our moods are very obedient to it." The wind and the air, the landscape, the light, the weather, the season, the time of day—all these factors combined with the walker's own attitude and outlook to affect the quality and nature of his intellectual and emotional life.

When Thoreau traversed the landscape, the external environment affected his inner self by touching all aspects of his being: physical, emotional, intellectual, and spiritual. He experienced nature at all these levels. At the physical and emotional level, Thoreau enjoyed a powerful sensual intercourse with nature. His walks were highly sensual affairs that sent him into very stimulated emotional states. Emerson wrote in *Nature* that "the lover of nature is he whose inward and outward senses are still truly adjusted to each other. . . . His intercourse with heaven and earth becomes part of his daily food."

Thoreau was the perfect fulfillment of this description. He coveted those experiences in which the walker "sees, hears, scents, tastes, and feels only himself,—the phenomena that show themselves in him,—his expanding body, his intellect and heart." According to Channing, Thoreau "was in the habit of saying,—Give me healthy senses, let me be thoroughly alive, and breathe freely in the very floodtide of the living world." In his *Journal*

Thoreau declares: "I must walk more with free senses." In a different entry (Princeton) he claims that "in health all the senses are indulged and each seeks its own gratification.—it is a pleasure to see, and to walk, and to hear."

When Thoreau used his senses to unlock the mysteries of the outer world, he better understood his inner world: "With our senses applied to the surrounding world we are reading our own physical and corresponding moral revolutions." He often achieved a remarkable sensual connection between his inner state and the external world. Such a situation is described in *Walden*, where he writes: "This is a delicious evening, when the whole body is one sense, and imbibes delight through every pore. I go and come with a strange liberty in Nature, a part of herself. As I walk along the stony shore of the pond in my shirt sleeves, though it is cool as well as cloudy and windy, and I see nothing special to attract me, all the elements are unusually congenial to me. The bullfrogs trump to usher in the night, and the note of the whip-poorwill is borne on the rippling wind from over the water. Sympathy with the fluttering alder and poplar leaves almost takes away my breath; yet, like the lake, my serenity is rippled but not ruffled." As in this instance Thoreau's senses acted like strings emotionally tying his inner landscape to the external one.

Because walking enabled Thoreau to confront directly the objective world with his senses, he freely applied his senses to varying landscapes and conditions. One *Journal* account reveals the active role his senses played in his explorations: "I still recall to mind that characteristic winter eve of December 9th; the cold, dry, and wholesome diet my mind and senses necessarily fed on." In *The Maine Woods* he records: "After a dinner . . . I walked across the clearing into the forest, southward, returning along the shore. For my dessert, I helped myself to a large slice of the Chesuncook woods, and took a hearty draught of its waters with all my senses."

Thoreau's sensual probing of the external world provided him with exhilarating carpe diem experiences. His commitment to experiencing life in the present is especially clear in this *Journal* proclamation: "The moods and thoughts of man are revolving just as steadily and incessantly as nature's. Nothing must be postponed. Take time by the forelock. Now or never! You must live in the present, launch yourself on every wave, find your eternity in each moment." The opening stanza of Thoreau's poem "Carpe Diem" preaches the same thought:

> Build not on to-morrow,
>   But seize on to-day!
> From no future borrow,
>   The present to pay.

Thoreau states in "Walking" that "we cannot afford not to live in the present," and his walks captured the magic of a given moment each time that his senses connected him to the immediacy of his surroundings.

In his *Journal* Thoreau recorded his desire to "be intoxicated on air and water!" Like Emily Dickinson, whose sensual ecstasy in nature was expressed in these lines— "Inebriate of Air—am I—/ And Debauchee of Dew—", Thoreau found himself during his walks sensually stimulated to the point of natural intoxication: "Each sight and sound and scent and flavor,—intoxicates with a healthy intoxication. . . . After I had been eating these simple wholesome, ambrosial fruits on this high hillside, I found my senses whetted, I was young again, and whether I stood or sat I was not the same creature."

Such sensual encounters with nature during his ramblings could transport Thoreau to a state of utter rapture. During one August hike, he found himself overcome by sense stimulation as the external environment lifted his mood and transformed him: "Each sound seems to come from out a greater thoughtfulness in nature, as if nature had acquired some character and mind. The cricket, the gurgling stream, the rushing wind amid the trees, all speak to me soberly yet encouragingly of the steady onward progress of the universe. My heart leaps into my mouth at the sound of the wind in the woods. I, whose life was but yesterday so desultory and shallow, suddenly recover my spirits, my spirituality, through my hearing. . . . Now I have occasion to be grateful for the flood of life that is flowing over me. I am not so poor: I can smell the ripening apples; the very rills are deep; the autumnal flowers . . . feed my spirit, endear the earth to me, make me value myself and rejoice; the quivering of pigeons' wings reminds me of the tough fibre of the air which they rend. I thank you, God. . . . I am impure and worthless, and yet the world is gilded for my delight and holidays are prepared for me, and my path is strewn with flowers. . . . It seems to me that I am more rewarded for my expectations than for anything I do or can do. Ah, I would not tread on a cricket in whose song is such a revelation, so soothing and cheering to my ear! Oh, keep my senses pure!"

The varied sights, sounds, scents, tastes, and textures that the natural world offered bridged the gap between nature and Thoreau's spirit. In typical transcendental fashion, Thoreau continually sought correspondences between the external landscape and his own internal landscape, and his senses provided him with the material for such correspondences.

During a walk Thoreau utilized every sense to ensure the most meaningful contact with nature, but he was probably more affected by his sense of hearing than by any other sense. When walking, he was easily transported into an ecstatic state upon hearing particular sounds. Commenting on this in his *Journal*, he notes: "There are few sounds still which never fail to affect me. The notes of the wood thrush and the sound of a vibrating chord, these affect me as many sounds once did often, and as almost all should. . . . They intoxicate, they charm us. . . . I would be drunk, drunk, dead drunk to this world with it forever. He that hath ears to hear, let him hear. The contact of sound with a human ear whose hearing is pure and unimpaired is coincident with an ecstasy. Sugar is not so sweet to the palate, as sound to the healthy ear; the hearing of it makes men brave."

The note of any bird often lifted his spirits and renewed him. Such was the case when, walking one day, he heard the cheery note of a bobolink. His response—"Methinks they are the most *liquidly* sweet and melodious sounds I ever heard. They are refreshing to my ear as the first distant tinkling and gurgling of a rill to a thirsty man"— indicates the power of the bird's song over him. Overcome, he remarked: "It is the foretaste of such strains as never fell on mortal ears, to hear which we should to our doors and contribute all that we possess or are." Appropriately, Thoreau used a bird's song as the focal point in his poem "The Cliffs & Springs," in which he presents the walker, moved by a veery's song, launched into a timeless, spaceless state of rapture:

When breathless noon hath paused on hill and vale,
. . . .
Somewhat it is, sole sojourner on earth,
To hear the verry on her oaken perch
Ringing her modest trill—
Sole sound of all the din that makes a world,
And I sole ear.
Fondly to nestle me in that sweet melody,
And own a kindred soul, speaking to me
From out the depths of universal being.

O'er birch and hazel, through the sultry air,
Comes that faint sound this way,
On Zephyr borne, straight to my ear.
No longer time or place, nor faintest trace
Of earth, the landscape's shimmer is my only space,
Sole remnant of a world.
Anon that throat has done, and familiar sounds
Swell strangely on the breeze, the low of cattle,
And the novel cries of sturdy swains
That plod the neighboring vale—
And I walk once more confounded a denizen of earth.

Sounds put Thoreau closer in touch with himself. When he sauntered in winter, the stillness freed him to hear himself better: "Then there is the wonderful stillness of a winter day. The sources of sound, as of water, are frozen up. . . . When we listen, we hear only that sound of the surf of our internal sea, rising and swelling in our ears as in two seashells." The sounds projected by a brook had much the same effect, especially during a night walk: "I hear the sound of Heywood's Brook falling into Fair Haven Pond, inexpressibly refreshing to my senses. It seems to flow through my very bones. I hear it with insatiable thirst. It allays some sandy heat in me. It affects my circulations; methinks my arteries have sympathy with it. What is it I hear but the pure waterfalls within me, in the circulation of my blood, the streams that fall into my heart? What mists do I ever see but such as hang over and rise from my blood? The sound of this gurgling water, running thus by night as by day, falls on all my dashes, fills all my buckets, overflows my float-boards, turns all the machinery of my nature, makes me a flume, a sluice-way, to the springs of nature. Thus I am washed; thus I drink and quench my thirst."

As with hearing, Thoreau had a strong sense of sight. He determined to glean visually all that he could from nature—"That I might never be blind to the beauty of the landscape"—and he was as easily intoxicated by what he saw as by what he heard: "In all my rambles I have seen no landscape which can make me forget Fair Haven. . . . The sight of these budding woods intoxicates me,— this diet drink." Seeing a bird, like hearing one, excited Thoreau. When during one walk he spotted a scarlet tanager contrasted with the green trees and blue sky, he observed: "I am transported; these are not the woods I ordinarily walk in. . . . How he enhances the wildness and wealth of the woods!"

Sight, like sound, propels the saunterer within himself. While walking one day, Thoreau observed the rich red color of polk berries and found himself moved from within—"It speaks to my blood." Even seeing something as common as speckled briar leaves in the fall affected his emotions and his thoughts: "It excites me to a sort of autumnal madness. They are leaves for Satyrus and Faunus to make their garlands of. My thoughts break out like them, spotted all over, yellow and green and brown."

Thoreau used his sense of sight to strengthen his relationship with nature, to match his own experience to her experience. Seeing a "faint tinge of green" in the spring landscape excited Thoreau, inviting him to join in the spirit of nature's triumph over winter: "I revive with Nature; her victory is mine. This is my jewelry." In "Autumnal Tints" Thoreau found his moods corresponding to the immediate environment in the fall as well, when the sight of nature's "annual fair in October" stunned his visual senses and lifted his spirits: "Did not all these [manifestations of fall color] suggest that man's spirits should rise as high as Nature's,—should hang out their flag, and the routine of his life be interrupted by an analogous expression of joy and hilarity?"

Thoreau's sense of smell, though not as strong as his

sense of hearing and sense of sight, also connected him to the natural world: "There are odors enough in nature to remind you of everything, if you had lost every sense but smell." As he rambled, he sniffed through the environment in primitive fashion: "Methinks the scent is a more primitive inquisition than the eye, more oracular and trustworthy. . . . The scent reveals, of course, what is concealed from the other senses. By it I detect earthiness." As with seeing and hearing, smelling certain things could intoxicate Thoreau: "As I walked, I was intoxicated with the slight spicy odor of the hickory buds and the bruised bark of the black birch, and, in the fall, the pennyroyal." Overcome by the scent of flowers in a field, Thoreau wrote: "If the air here always possessed this bland sweetness, this spot would become famous and be visited by sick and well from all parts of the earth. It would be carried off in bottles and become an article of traffic which kings would strive to monopolize. The air of Elysium cannot be more sweet."

Thoreau's sense of smell put him in touch with nature in a very personal way, allowing him to match his experience with that of nature and to identify with her moods. One can see this in his *Journal* account of a September night hike: "How much excited we are, how much recruited, by a great many particular fragrances! A field of ripening corn, now at night, that has been topped, with the stalks stacked up to dry,—an inexpressibly dry, rich, sweet, ripening scent. I feel as if I were an ear of ripening corn myself." Thoreau contended that as long as the body functioned and allowed him to explore sensually his surroundings, to sniff and smell nature's odors, he would feel a correspondence with nature that would affect his own experience: "I still perceive that ambrosial sweetness from the meadows in some places. Give me strong, rank scent of ferns in the spring for vigor; just blossoming late in the spring. A healthy and refined nature would always derive pleasure from the landscape. As long as the bodily vigor lasts, man sympathizes with nature."

Of all his senses, taste and touch were Thoreau's weakest. Still, he related to his environment with these senses in the same way as the others, with much the same results. His walks were filled with opportunities to taste or to touch things, and such encounters affected the quality and nature of his walking experiences. Thoreau could sip the sap flowing from scarlet oaks during a November walk and note its "pleasantly astringent taste, this strong oak wine." He could enjoy the spicy taste of fever-bush berries and find himself so affected as to be transported "in thought to the spice islands." The taste of tart cranberries could infuse him with vigor: "No tarts that I ever tasted at any table ever possessed such a refreshing, cheering, encouraging acid that literally put the heart in you and set you on edge for this world's experiences, bracing the spirit."

Touch affected him in a similar fashion, connecting his body to the landscape and altering his inner life. In his *Journal* he mused: "My body is all sentient. As I go here or there, I am tickled by this or that I come in contact with, as if I touched the wires of a battery. I can generally recall—have fresh in my mind—several scratches last received. These I continually recall to mind, reimpress, and harp upon." Making physical contact with nature bonded it to him; when grasping objects during his walk, he was often reluctant to release them: "Acorns, red and white . . . , appear to be fallen or falling. They are so fair and plump and glossy that I love to handle them, and am loath to throw away what I have in my hand."

Thoreau's sensual interaction with nature was, like the other aspects of his walking experience, thorough and deep. Walking allowed him to place his body in any situation that might appeal to his senses; and so, as he explored to discover the external features of the landscape, he used his senses to cultivate a personal relationship with nature, to match his experience with her own, and to connect his inner life with the external phenomena that his senses probed.

Thoreau sought in nature a companion and friend. This is not to suggest that he was misanthropic, for Thoreau had his share of human friends and valued human contact. But Thoreau held a special regard for nature as well, and his desire to make contact with her was fulfilled by the walks he took. It was necessary for Thoreau to internalize the landscape, to feel with and respond to his external surroundings. "It is in vain to write on the seasons unless you have the seasons in you," he wrote in his *Journal*, and the use of his senses while sauntering made such internalization possible as sense stimulation was converted to emotional and intellectual response.

Because of his desire to interact with and relate to nature, Thoreau did not go on a walk for the sake of observation alone. The ultimate purpose of his walks was to completely open himself up to nature's influences, to walk in such a way that nature reached him through his senses and touched his inner being. "Live in each season as it passes; breathe the air, drink the drink, taste the fruit, and resign yourself to the influences of each. Let them be your only diet drink and botanical medicines. . . . Be blown on by all the winds. Open all your pores and bathe in all the tides of Nature, in all her streams and oceans, at all seasons."

Thoreau vowed to immerse himself in nature, to acquire a "living sense" of the landscape he traversed. As he sauntered, he would "taste the world and digest it," he would become "part and parcel of Nature."

Eating offered Thoreau one way to internalize nature. In his *Journal* he describes a July walk during which he paused from a surveying job to eat raw turnips. Equating this action with the eating habits of cows, he identified himself with their primitive appetites and characteristics: "I, too, tried hard to chew a mouthful of raw turnips and realize the life of cows and oxen. . . . These are things which travellers do. How many men have tasted raw turnips! How many have eaten a whole one! Some bovine appetites, which find some fodder in every field."

Eating the natural food like these turnips that was available during a walk offered Thoreau an opportunity to enjoy a very special relationship with nature: "Nature does her best to feed man. The traveller need not go out of the road to get as many [berries] as he wants; every bush and vine teems with palatable fruit. Man for once stands in such relation to Nature as the animals that pluck and eat as they go. . . . We pluck and eat in remembrance of her. It is a sacrament, a communion. . . . Slight and innocent savors, which relate us to Nature, make us her guests and entitle us to her regard and protection."

Just the act of picking berries, while rambling through the fields, provided Thoreau with special experiences that reinforced his bond with nature. His *Journal* recollection of a July berry-picking adventure reveals the value he placed in the activity of picking the berries: "I got invaluable experience beside! A half a day of liberty like that was like the promise of eternal life. It was emancipation in New England. O, what a day was there, my countrymen!" In a much later *Journal* entry he emphasizes the same quality of experience: "When I used to pick the berries for dinner on the East Quarter hills I did not eat one till I had done, for going a-berrying implies more things than eating the berries. They at home got only the pudding: I got the forenoon out of doors, and the appetite for the pudding." The activity involved in berry-picking could naturally alter Thoreau's mood: "The slight distraction of picking berries is favorable to a mild, abstracted, poetic mood, to sequestered or transcendental thinking. I return even more fresh to my mood from such slight interruptions."

Whether picking or eating berries during his rambles, Thoreau considered the immediate environment an important factor for determining the quality of his berrying experiences. Eating could affect the walker's feelings about his environment and aid his adjustment to a new environment. He describes this effect in "A Walk to Wachusett," where he notes how gathering and eating berries as he climbed to a higher elevation helped him adjust to the more elevated environment: "As we gathered the raspberries, which grew abundantly by the roadside, we fancied that that action was consistent with a lofty prudence; as if the traveler who ascends into a mountainous region should fortify himself by eating of such light ambrosial fruits as grow there, and drinking of the springs which gush out from the mountain-sides, as he gradually inhales the subtler and purer atmosphere of those elevated places, thus propitiating the mountain gods by a sacrifice of their own fruit. The gross products of the plains and valleys are for such as dwell therein; but it seemed to us that the juices of this berry had relation to the thin air of the mountain tops."

Ever aware of the interactions between the walker, the environment, and the walking situation, Thoreau repeatedly notes the influences of the environment on the quality of the saunterer's personal experience.

No matter what is eaten, Thoreau discovered that the environment affects the quality of the taste of the food the walker consumes. According to Thoreau, in a natural setting food tastes better and retains its original flavor; in a foreign or civilized setting, food loses its flavor and inspirational quality. In *Walden* he writes: "The fruits do not yield their true flavor to the purchaser of them, nor to him who raises them for the market. There is but one way to obtain it, yet few take that way. If you would know the flavor of huckleberries, ask the cow-boy or the partridge. It is a vulgar error to suppose that you have tasted huckleberries who never plucked them." The combination of the walker's own exertion—picking the berry—with the value of the natural landscape preserves the fruit's true flavor. The saunterer's appetite is different from anyone else's because only he earns his food by gleaning it himself and eating it in its natual setting: "The farmer thinks . . . he has better [wild apples] in his barrels, but he is mistaken, unless he has a walker's appetite and imagination, neither of which can he have. . . . The saunterer's apple not even the saunterer can eat in the house."

In "Wild Apples" Thoreau explains more fully why the saunterer must eat his apples outdoors and how doing so enhances his experience: "To appreciate the wild and sharp flavors of these October fruits, it is necessary that you be breathing the sharp October or November air. The outdoor air and exercise which the walker gets give a different tone to his palate, and he craves a fruit which the sedentary would call harsh and crabbed. They must be eaten in the fields, when your system is all aglow with exercise, when the frosty weather nips your fingers, the wind rattles the bare boughs or rustles the few remaining leaves, and the jay is heard screaming around. What is sour in the house a bracing walk makes sweet. Some of these apples might be labeled, 'To be eaten in the wind.'"

Thoreau adds, "In the fields only are the sours and bitters of Nature appreciated." He had to be in the fields in order to experience what nature had to offer him. Thoreau walked into nature, enjoying its tastes in natural settings, eating whatever would help him satisfy his striking appetite to experience nature sensually.

Thoreau's walks involved an effort to "eat" nature, to taste, chew, and assimilate it into his own blood stream. Nothing was exempt from Thoreau's appetite, not even the earth's crust: "I was drawn toward and worshipped the brownish light in the sod,—the withered grass, etc., on barren hills. I felt as if I could eat the very crust of the earth; I never felt so terrene, never sympathized so with the surface of the earth."

Drinking, like eating, allowed Thoreau to establish sensually a personal relationship with nature while he walked in it. As with eating, taking liquid into one's self from nature's natural supply affects the inner life of the walker, much as a child drinking from his mother's breast. Thoreau's *Journal* account of one walk during which he drank from a spring illustrates this: "I lie almost flat, resting my hands on what offers, to drink at this water where it bubbles, at the very udders of Nature, for man is never weaned from her breast while this life lasts—How many times in a single walk does he stoop for a draught!" Water, once assimilated into the saunterer's body, works its magic on him, affecting him with the purifying and inspirational qualities that it possesses in its natural state. Such was the experience Thoreau had during a night walk: "Nut Meadow Brook where it crosses the road beyond Jenny Dugan's that was. I do not drink in vain. I mark that brook as if I had swallowed a water snake that would live in my stomach. I have swallowed something worth the while. The day is not what it was before I stooped to drink. . . . There were some seeds of thought, methinks, floating in that water, which are expanding in me. The man must not drink of the running streams, the living waters, who is not prepared to have all nature reborn in him,—to suckle monsters."

Thoreau was particularly affected by drinking birch sap: "Suppose we were to drink only the yellow birch sap and mix its bark with our bread, would not its yellow curls sprout from our foreheads, and our breath and persons exhale its sweet aroma? What sappy vigor there would be in our limbs! What sense we should have to explore the swamps with!" As with eating fruits, the effect of the liquid on the saunterer depends on the environment—the more natural the environment, the stronger the effect. Thus "like wild apples, [birch sap] must be tasted in the fields, and then it has a very slightly sweetish and acid taste, and cool as iced water."

During particularly warm weather, Thoreau not only established a relationship with nature by eating and drinking, he also bathed in ponds, streams, and rivers, sharing the same water as the wild creatures and allowing the water to cool and refresh himself. During one August ramble, Thoreau bathed in a local stream and then recorded: "With what sober joy I stand to let the water drip from me and feel my fresh vigor, who have been bathing in the same tub which the muskrat uses! Such a medicated bath as only nature furnishes."

Even as Thoreau felt bovine in his appetite, he felt amphibious in his desire to bathe during a walk: "Men are inclined to be amphibious, to sympathize with fishes, now. I desire to get wet and saturated with water." Bathing made him feel like an accepted part of nature, like one of her own creatures who inhabited the same waters. One bath caused him to conclude: "I begin to inhabit the planet, and see how I may be naturalized at last." To enter the water was a baptismal rite for Thoreau; the water readily assimilated him into nature and made him feel part of her: "Though the river is thus high, we bathe at Cardinal Shore and find the water unexpectedly warm and the air also delicious. Thus we are baptized into nature."

Water, like air, could be assimilated into the walker's system; it offered the rambler the opportunity to become one with the environment. When Thoreau walked along the shore of Cape Cod, he "determined to get it into" him. In *A Week* he notes how when he hiked into swamps, he wanted to become one with the swamp: "I

97

can fancy that it would be a luxury to stand up to one's chin in some retired swamp a whole summer day, scenting the wild honeysuckle and bilberry blows, and lulled by the minstrelsy of gnats and mosquitoes! . . . — Surely one may as profitably be soaked in the juices of a swamp for one day as pick his way dry-shod over sand. Cold and damp,—are they not as rich experience as warmth and dryness?''

Wading in a swamp, like bathing in a river, often refreshed Thoreau and spiritualized his experience: "I wade in the swamp. . . . The water is now gratefully cool to my legs, so far from being poisoned in the strong water of the swamp. It is a sort of baptism for which I had waited.''

Such experiences suggest one of the real advantages of walking to a naturist like Thoreau; walking helped him immerse himself in the landscape, to experience it in all its forms. These sensual experiences appealed to his body as much as to his mind or soul. The sense appeals offered by nature wooed his body, and water, in particular, offered physical rejuvenation. A *Journal* entry recounts, "We find it delicious to take off our shoes and stockings and wade far through the shallows on the meadow to the Bedford shore, to let our legs drink air.''

Thoreau enjoyed such physical refreshment when he chose to walk through rivers and streams instead of just bathing in them. This water sauntering offered Thoreau a luxurious sense experience: "I wonder if any Roman emperor ever indulged in such luxury as this,—of walking up and down a river in torrid weather with only a hat to shade the head. What were the baths of Caracalla to this? . . . On this road there is no other traveller to turn out for.'' Thoreau coveted these water-walking experiences, but he knew that the conditions had to be just right for him to realize the physically stimulating response that such walking made possible: "That the luxury of walking in the river may be perfect it must be very warm, such as are few days even in July, so that the breeze on those parts of the body that have just been immersed may not produce the least chilliness. It cannot be too warm, so that, with a shirt to fend the sun from your back, you may walk with perfect indifference, or rather with equal pleasure, alternately in deep and in shallow water. Both water and air must be unusually warm; otherwise we shall feel no impulse to cast ourselves into and remain in the stream. To-day it is uncomfortably cool for such a walk."

With the right conditions, a fluvial excursion could provide the walker with the perfect balance between walking as an act of discovery and walking as sense experience: "Now for another fluvial walk. . . . Divesting yourself of all clothing but your shirt and hat, which are to protect your exposed parts from the sun, you are prepared for the fluvial excursion. You choose what depths you like, tucking your toga higher or lower, as you take the deep middle of the road or the shallow sidewalks. . . . Now your feet expand on a smooth sandy bottom, now contract timidly on pebbles, now slump in genial fatty mud— greasy, saponaceous—amid the pads. You scare out whole schools of small breams and perch, and sometimes a pickerel, which have taken shelter from the sun under the pads. . . . Or you meet with and interrupt a turtle taking a more leisurely walk up the stream. . . . In shallow water near the shore, your feet at once detect the presence of springs in the bank emptying in, by the sudden coldness of the water, and there, if you are thirsty, you dig a little well in the sand with your hands, and when you return, after it has settled and clarified itself, get a draught of pure cold water there."

In any form, moisture appealed to Thoreau. Getting wet strengthened his relationship with nature and touched his inner life. Water, like the spirit of nature itself, penetrated his skin and altered his personal experience:

"To get the value of the storm we must be out a long time and travel far in it, so that it may fairly penetrate our skin, and we be as it were turned inside out to it, and there be no part in us but is wet or weather-beaten,—so that we become storm men instead of fair-weather men." Just the act of walking in the rain affected Thoreau's thoughts and feelings; the contact of the rain with his skin corresponded with a much deeper contact of nature with his psychological self: "You feel the fertilizing influence of the rain in your mind. The part of you that is wettest is fullest of life, like the lichens."

The land, as well as the water, offered Thoreau ample opportunities to relate sensually to the environment as he walked through it, strengthening in the process his relationship with nature and affecting the quality of his inner experience. He was as determined to get the earth into himself as he was to assimilate water: "You must love the crust of the earth on which you dwell more than the sweet crust of any bread or cake. You must be able to extract nutriment out of a sandheap. You must have so good an appetite as this, else you will live in vain." Any sensual contact with the ground or anything associated with the ground excited Thoreau: "The earth looks warm and genial again. . . . I could almost lie down in the furrow and be warmed into her life and growth."

Even wading through weeds and grass provided Thoreau with the opportunity to bond sensually with the environment—a terrestrial counterpart to his fluvial excursions: "We walked in some trodden path on account of the wet grass and leaves, but the fine grass overhanging paths, weighed down with dewy rain, wet our feet nevertheless. We cannot afford to omit seeing the beaded grass and wetting our feet." Thoreau even wrote a poem to commemorate this kind of walking experience. He celebrates the walker's contact with weeds and flowers, and the pollen and dust they cast on the walker's shoes, as the mark that distinguishes the genuine walker from those who never walk through the fields. This latter group is only "transported" from place to place rather than traveling like Thoreau through nature and making contact with it:

Tall Ambrosia
Among the signs of autumn I perceive
The Roman wormwood . . .
. . . .
Sprinkles its yellow dust over my shoes
As I cross the now neglected garden
—We trample under foot the food of gods
& spill their nectar in each drop of dew—
My honest shoes Fast friends that never stray
far from my couch thus powdered countryfied
Bearing many a mile the marks of their adventure
At the post-house disgrace the Gallic gloss
Of those well dressed ones who no morning dew
Nor Roman wormwood ever have been through
Who never walk but are *transported* rather—
For what old crime of theirs I do not gather.

As with water sauntering, walking on land allows the traveler to confront nature sensually without interference and to merge himself with the landscape, identifying with her moods and qualities. Traveling through weeds could accomplish this for the saunterer as well as wading through a meadow: "The weeds begin to be high in low grounds and low wood-path . . . suggesting a certain fecundity and vigor in nature, so that we love to wade through their ranks." Walking on the land, as with water-sauntering, was a completely participatory act for Thoreau. He valued any interaction with nature, and walking provided him with numerous ways that he could participate in nature's processes, including the inadvertent spreading of seeds: "Perhaps Nature would condescend to make use of us even without our knowledge, as when we help to scatter her seeds in our walks, and carry burrs and cockles on our clothes from field to field."

At the most basic level of experience of Thoreau's sauntering adventures, he walked in nature, sensually probing it and actively attempting to assimilate the environment into himself. Whether eating, drinking, bathing, or hiking, Thoreau found his walks filled with opportunities to interact sensually with the environment and, in the process, to enhance his special relationship with nature.

Walking, however, provided Thoreau with other types of experiences. At a different and perhaps higher level from his sense experience, walking was a very heroic, adventurous act that fed his desire to live a courageous, moral life in a world ruled by the mundane and unheroic. In his *Journal* (Princeton), he describes the tension within himself between the contemplative and the active life— "The struggle in me is between a love of contemplation and a love of action—the life of a philosopher & of a hero," and walking was one important way that he fulfilled the active, heroic side of his personality. Influenced by the *Bhagavad-Gita* as well as by his own New England temperament, Thoreau found real satisfaction in living the kind of active life that walking made possible: "It is good policy to be stirring about your affairs, for the reward of activity and energy is that if you do not accomplish the object you had professed to yourself, you do accomplish something else. So, in any natural history walks, it commonly turns out that, going for one thing, I get another."

Thoreau viewed the walks he took in nature as heroic quests that set him apart from his contemporaries who remained in town or near to home and lived dull and uneventful lives. In *Walden* he writes: "Men come tamely home at night from the next field or street, where their household echoes haunt, and their life pines because it breathes its own breath over again; their shadows morning and evening reach farther than their daily steps. We should come home from far, from adventures, and perils, and discoveries every day, with new experience and character."

For Thoreau, walking was a quest for adventure and honor, an activity that offered the saunterer an opportunity to experience the heroic and the chivalric. In his essay "Walking" he observes: "It is true, we are but faint-hearted crusaders, even the walkers, nowadays, who undertake no persevering, never-ending enterprises. Our expeditions are but tours, and come round again at evening to the old hearth-side from which we set out. Half the walk is but retracing our steps. We should go forth on the shortest walk, perchance, in the spirit of undying adventure, never to return,—prepared to send back our embalmed hearts only as relics to our desolate kingdoms. / To come down to my own experience, my companion and I, for I sometimes have a companion, take pleasure in fancying ourselves knights of a new, or rather an old, order,—not Equestrians or Chevaliers, not Ritters or Riders, but Walkers, a still more ancient and honorable class, I trust. The chivalric and heroic spirit which once belonged to the Rider seems now to reside in, or perchance to have subsided into, the Walker."

Here Thoreau presents the chivalric aspects of his saunterings, not dealing with a tournament for the hand of a fair maiden, but anticipating the many adventures a walk could offer one who entered it in the right spirit and who gave himself in chivalric fashion to the female principle of the landscape. The physical rigors of the walk, the difficulty of the terrain, the challenges posed by the environment and the walking situation, the mysteries of the exploration—these provide the saunterer with the chivalric quest he seeks. Thus Thoreau proposed a new form of chivalry, one based upon the walker who saunters with a spirit of adventure and expectation, a man who owes no allegiance to any lord, but seeks only the rewards offered by his walking experiences.

According to Thoreau, "a little adventure like a walk" could convert an ordinary winter landscape into the opportunity for chivalric experience: "Now for a brisk and energetic walk, with a will and a purpose. Have done with sauntering, in the idle sense. You must rush to the assault of winter. Make haste into the outskirts, climb the ramparts of the town, be on the alert and let nothing escape your observations." Any contact with nature during a walk had an adventurous quality to it, as the time when Thoreau found himself "covered with seeds," which had stuck to him during a walk. He considered these green seeds which covered his legs "a kind of coat of mail. It was the event of our walk, and we were proud to wear this badge, as if he were the most distinguished who had the most on his clothes." Even when Thoreau reminisced about walking, he often did so in chivalric terms. In a letter to Ralph Waldo Emerson and his wife, Thoreau wrote: "And Hawthorne too I remember as one with whom I sauntered in old heroic times along the banks of the Scamander [Concord], amid the ruins of chariots and heroes."

Thoreau's writings are full of references to his desire to experience adventure during his saunterings. A walk was never fully satisfying to him unless it contained an element of danger or adventure. Although Thoreau eagerly anticipated the discoveries that he hoped to make during a walk, it was the adventure and excitement of the walk itself that most satisfied him. In a letter to his good friend H. G. O. Blake, Thoreau revealed his enthusiasm for the element of adventure in his sauntering experiences. In describing his climb of Mount Monadnock, Thoreau shared with Blake the inhospitable conditions under which the initial ascent took place. According to Thoreau, the climb, subject to wild, stormy weather, "was a great deal better than going up there in fair weather, & having no adventure . . . but dull common-place sleep in a useless house, & before a comparatively useless fire—such as we get every night." In an earlier letter to Blake, Thoreau had noted that a previous mountain ramble had not been that satisfying because "the mode of it was not simple and adventurous enough."

The more difficult and challenging the walk, the more Thoreau valued it. He found himself drawn to wild, in-hospitable landscapes. At one point in *The Maine Woods* he recounts how he and his Indian guide surveyed dis-tant "solemn bear-haunted mountains." The threatening nature of this landscape enticed him: "My imagination personified the slopes themselves, as if by their very length they would waylay you, and compel you to camp again on them before night. Some invisible glutton would seem to drop from the trees and gnaw at the heart of the solitary hunter who threaded those woods; and yet I was tempted to walk there."

Emerson had exclaimed, "The characteristic of heroism is its persistency"; and Thoreau cherished the heroic na-ture of any walk that tested his persistency and chal-lenged him physically and mentally. He seemed espe-cially proud of the physically challenging walking that he did and recorded in his *Journal* the details of a hike that he claimed was representative of his local rambles: "Would it not be well to describe some of those rough all-day walks across lots?—as that of the 15th, picking our way over quaking meadows and swamps and occasionally slipping into the muddy batter midleg deep; jumping or fording ditches and brooks; forcing our way through dense blueberry swamps, where there is water beneath and bushes above; then brushing through extensive birch forests all covered with green lice, which cover our clothes and face; then, relieved, under larger wood, more open beneath, steering for some more conspicuous trunk; now along a rocky hillside where the sweet-fern grows for a mile, then over a recent cutting, finding our uncertain footing on the cracking tops and trimmings of trees left by the choppers; now taking a step or two of smooth walking across a highway; now through a dense pine wood, descending into a rank, dry swamp, where the cinnamon fern rises above your head, with isles of poison-dogwood; now up a scraggy hill covered with shrub oak, stooping and winding one's way for half a mile, tearing one's clothing in many places and putting out one's eyes, and find[ing] at last that it has no bare brow, but another slope of the same character; now through a corn-field diagonally with the rows; now coming upon the hidden melon-patch; seeing the back side of familiar hills and not knowing them,—the nearest house to home, which you do not know . . .; now reaching on higher land some open pigeon-place, a breathing-place for us." Such a description leaves the reader winded, gasping for breath, but this kind of walking invigorated Thoreau, providing him with adventure.

His writings contain numerous descriptions of the physical challenges of walks that would have intimidated all but the most dedicated saunterer. Thoreau describes several of these rigorous walking adventures in *The Maine Woods*, such as this sample passage: "The walking rapidly grew worse, and the path more indistinct, and at length . . . we found ourselves in a more open and regular swamp, made less passable than ordinary by the unusual wetness of the season. We sank a foot deep in water and mud at every step, and sometimes up to our knees, and the trail was almost obliterated, being no more than that a musquash leaves in similar places, when he parts the floating sedge. . . . It would have been amusing to behold the dogged and deliberate pace at which we entered that swamp, without interchanging a word, as if determined to go through it, though it should come up to our necks." As in this description, Thoreau liked to draw the reader's attention to the heroic nature of his sauntering struggles.

Thoreau's walks helped him identify with the adventurous among his countrymen, those who were willing to take risks and respond to challenges. While his contemporaries demonstrated their courage and initiative in other ways, Thoreau used walking as the means to assert his own heroic nature: "The timid or ill-shod confine themselves to the land side, where they get comparatively few berries and many scratches, but the more adventurous, making their way through the open swamp . . . obtain access to those great drooping clusters of berries which no hand has disturbed."

Thoreau often went out of his way to ensure that his walking experience would provide him with the challenges that he thrived on. He typically charted difficult routes for his walks and shunned easy passages that might deprive him of adventure and excitement. In *A Week* Thoreau's plans for one hike reveal this tendency: "But I determined to follow up the valley to its head, and then find my own route up the steep, as the shorter and more adventurous way." It was Thoreau's custom to select a destination and then to head cross-country, sticking to a straight line until he reached his objective. According to legend, Thoreau and a hiking companion once walked through a farmhouse rather than detour around it, leaving the shocked family sitting stunned at their dining table. William Channing's description of Thoreau's orientation process emphasizes the heroic nature of his approach: "He ascended such hills as Monadnoc or Saddleback Mountain by his own path; would lay down his map on the summit and draw a line to the point he proposed to visit below (perhaps forty miles away in the landscape), and set off bravely to make the short-cut. The lowland people wondered to see him scaling the heights as if he had lost his way, or at his 'jumping over their cow-yard fences,' asking if he had fallen from the clouds."

Although Thoreau's sense encounters with the landscape provided him with remarkable and stimulating experiences of the moment, his heroic walking adventures connected him with the past as well as the present, helping him to identify his own experiences with those of the pioneers who had lived before him. In *A Week* Thoreau explains the connection between one's personal experiences and history: "All the events which make the annals of the nations are but the shadows of our private experiences. . . . In other words, the history which we read is only a fainter memory of events which have happened in our own experience."

Thoreau's walking experience allowed him to live out history, to be one of the "sturdy pioneers," whom his *Journal* (Princeton) indicates he felt called to emulate. When Thoreau explored Cape Cod, he thought of the Pilgrims and wished to relive some of their experiences. When inland, he sought experiences that connected himself with the early settlers: "It is surprising how much room there is in nature,—if a man will follow his proper path. In these broad fields, in these extensive woods, on this stretching river, I never meet a walker. Passing behind the farmhouses, I see no man out. Perhaps I do not meet so many men as I should have met three centuries ago, when the Indian hunter roamed these woods. I enjoy the retirement and solitude of an early settler."

Just as Thoreau's travel reading expanded his microcosm and helped him universalize his sauntering discoveries, so his travel reading contributed to the quality of the walking experience itself, allowing him to identify his adventures with those he had read about. His *Journal* description of a particular winter hike demonstrates how this worked: "We crossed the Great Meadows lengthwise, a broad level plain, roughened only by snowy waves, about two miles long and nearly half as wide. Looking back over it made me think of what I have read of Arctic explorers travelling over snow-covered ice."

Although he was very interested in the life of the body, in how his walks provided him with sensual experiences and physical challenges, Thoreau was far more enthusiastic about the life of the mind and how his walks affected his own thinking processes. Intellectual experiences were more important to him than sensual or emotional ones. More than merely sensually absorbing the landscape within himself or experiencing firsthand the physical dangers and difficulties of walking, Thoreau sought during his saunterings to absorb cognitively the landscape, to drink and digest mentally all the surface features that he discovered. As Sherman Paul notes, such a process was truly transcendental: "As much of the external world as man transformed into himself and radiated with meaning, so much did he truly possess: and again, this was not knowledge, but an acquisition of being, an enlargement of self."

Thoreau most valued mental sauntering that corresponded to his physical walking. In his *Journal* he observes: "Why can we not oftener refresh one another with original thoughts? If the fragrance of the dicksonia fern is so grateful and suggestive to us, how much more refreshing and encouraging—recreating—would be fresh and fragrant thoughts communicated to us fresh from a man's experience and life! I want . . . that he should . . . as it were, [go] a-huckleberrying in the fields of thought, and enrich all the world with his visions and joys."

In *Walden* he emphasized his commitment to mental sauntering: "The intellect is a cleaver; it discerns and rifts its way into the secret of things. . . . My instinct tells me that my head is an organ for burrowing, as some creatures use their snout and fore-paws, and with it I would mine and burrow my way through these hills." Mental traveling within offered Thoreau the greatest possiblities for exploration. In his *Journal* (Princeton) he writes: "The landscape lies fair within. The deepest and most original thinker is the farthest travelled."

Such mental sauntering seemed more chivalric and heroic than the actual physical walking that Thoreau did. In one letter he wrote: "How you can overrun a country, climb any rampart, and carry any fortress, with an army of alert thoughts!—thoughts that sent their bullets home to heaven's door,—with which you can take the whole world, without paying for it, or robbing anybody. See, the conquering hero comes! You fail in your thoughts, or you prevail in your thoughts only."

Thoreau believed that the exploration of the external landscape accompanied a more important exploration of the internal landscape: "Men have circumnavigated the globe of land and water, but how few have sailed out of sight of common sense over the ocean of knowledge!" The world of the self supplanted the world of nature as Thoreau sauntered about. His final focus was always within, on his deepest thoughts and feelings; this inner landscape interested him most.

Thoreau sounded the call to explore the inner landscape in *Walden:* "Nay, be a Columbus to whole new continents and worlds within you, opening new channels, not of trade, but of thought. Every man is the lord of a realm beside which the earthly empire of the Czar is but a petty state, a hummock left by the ice." He resolved in "Life Without Principle" to seek "the gold within me," and in his essay "Reform and Reformers" he establishes the importance of this inward quest: "Most whom I meet in the streets are, so to speak, outward bound, they live out and out, are going and coming, looking before and behind, all out of doors and in the air. I would fain see them inward bound, retiring in and in, farther and farther every day, and when I inquired for them I should not hear, that they had gone abroad anywhere . . . but that they had withdrawn deeper within the folds of being." Thoreau's statement in his *Journal*, "Let us migrate interiorly without intermission," charts the direction his walking experience took.

Thoreau's commitment to explore within raises the question of how walking helped him do this. The answer to this question deals in part with the complex relationship between body and mind. The walker is both head and body. His walking experience depends upon the cooperation between body and mind, a point Thoreau made in a letter to a friend: "Men should not labor foolishly like brutes, but the brain and the body should always, or as much as possible, work and rest together, and then the work will be of such a kind that when the body is hungry the brain will be hungry also, and the same food will suffice for both."

Thoreau saw a correspondence between the action of the body during walking and resulting mental activity: "The mind may perchance be persuaded to act, to energize, by the action and energy of the body. Any kind of liquid will fetch the pump." Walking offered the perfect activity to prime his mental pump and get his thoughts flowing. According to Thoreau, mental energy is dependent on physical energy: "Indeed, the mind never makes a great and successful effort without a corresponding energy of the body" (*A Week*). And he knew that a good mind was dependent upon a good body because of the energy level needed to walk and to think: "A man thinks as well through his legs and arms as his brain. We exaggerate the importance and exclusiveness of the headquarters. Do you suppose they were a race of consumptives and dyspeptics who invented Grecian mythology and po-etry? . . . I trust we have a good body then."

Emerson, Thoreau's friend and mentor, understood the relationship between body and mind. He held that "walking has the best value as gymnastics for the mind" ("Country Life"). Convinced that walking was the best activity for promoting spontaneous thinking, he stated in "Intellect": "Our spontaneous action is always the best. You cannot with your best deliberation and heed come so close to any question as your spontaneous glance shall bring you, whilst you rise from your bed, or walk abroad in the morning after meditating the matter before sleep on the previous night. . . . We do not determine what we will think," he adds. "We only open our senses, clear away as we can all obstruction from the fact, and suffer the intellect to see."

Thoreau valued spontaneous thoughts or impressions, and his writings, such as the following *Journal* entry, re-veal the greater importance of these insights over the more conscious, rational thoughts which he sometimes entertained: "I have thoughts, as I walk, on some subject that is running in my head, but all their pertinence seems gone before I can get home to set them down. The most valuable thoughts which I entertain are anything but what I thought. Nature abhors a vacuum, and if I can only walk with sufficient carelessness I am sure to be filled."

Walking helped Thoreau explore his mental landscape in several ways. In "Walking" he states, "You must walk life a camel, which is said to be the only beast which ruminates when walking"; and his walks were filled with his own special brand of ruminating. Walking afforded Thoreau the freedom to think so that his thoughts could transcend his immediate physcial surroundings and saunter in their own direction: "With what a breadth I advance! I am not bounded by the walks. I think more than the road full. . . . While I am abroad, the ovi-positors plant their seeds in me; I am fly-blown with thought, and go home to hatch and brood over them. . . . I was too discursive and rambling in my thought for the chamber, and must go where the wind blows on me walking."

When Thoreau's thoughts built up or seemed un-manageable, he walked to clear his head and mentally sort things out. In his *Journal* he notes that he "must get up earlier and take a morning walk" when he is mentally dammed up and "freighted with thought."

One aspect of the walking experience that nutured Thoreau's thinking was its privacy. The isolation of the walker, which he controls at will, makes private thoughts and reveries more possible than for those traveling in other ways: "In your thoughts no more than in your walks do you meet men. In moods I find such privacy as in dismal swamps and on mountain-tops."

The quiet, which the isolation of the walker makes pos-sible, also fostered Thoreau's mental sauntering. In a let-ter to his friend Blake, Thoreau described a world-ridden state that he wished to escape and recounted how walk-ing freed him from the "shallow din" that afflicted him so. He determined to "walk in various directions and see if there was not to be found any depth of silence around. As Bonaparte sent out his horsemen in the Red Sea on all sides to find shallow water, so I sent forth my mounted thoughts to find deep water."

Thoreau's *Journal* record of one saunter also reveals how the quiet and isolation of the walking experience led him from the world without to the world within: "I am soothed by the delicious stillness of the evening, save that on the hills the wind blows. I was surprised by the sound of my own voice. It is an atmosphere burden-some with thought. For the first time for a month, at least, I am reminded that thought is possible. The din of trivialness is silenced. I float over or through the deeps of silence."

The physical act of walking by itself cannot account for all of Thoreau's inward exploration. As with the other aspects of his sauntering experience, the walking environment affected him, influencing his moods and thoughts. Sense impressions sparked by the landscape not only stimulated Thoreau but triggered thoughts as well, as expressed in his *Journal:* "Most, if not all, . . . of our ideas may be due to some sort of sensuous impression of which we may or may not be conscious." When he walked, the action of the walk, the isolation and quiet, and the sense appeals of the environment combined to initiate thought and plunge Thoreau into his own private world.

Each type of environment affected his mental sauntering in a different way. Winter walking had its own special impact on his ability to explore his inner world. The harsh winter environment drove the saunterer's focus inward, contrasting each precious thought with the barrenness and bleakness of the landscape: "Friends long since gone there, and you left to walk on frozen ground, with your hands in your pockets. Ah, but is not this a glorious time for your deep inward fires? . . . True, the freezing ground is being prepared for immeasurable snows, but there are brave thoughts within you that shall remain to rustle the winter through like white oak leaves upon your boughs, or like scrub oaks that remind the traveller of a fire upon the hillsides; or evergreen thoughts, cold even in mid-summer, by their nature shall contrast the more fairly with the snow."

Cold weather draws the walker's attention away from natural phenomena and toward himself and his own ideas: "In this cold, clear, rough air from the northwest we walk amid what simple surroundings! Surrounded by our thoughts or imaginary objects, living in our ideas, not

114

one in a million ever sees the objects which are actually around him." Even the winter light has a special effect: "This clear, cold, November light is inspiriting. . . . Your thoughts sparkle like the water surface and the downy twigs." Another *Journal* entry reveals the effect of winter on one's thinking processes: "It took the cold and bleakness of November to ripen the walnut, but the human brain is the kernal which the winter itself matures. Not till then does its shell come off. . . . The winter was made to concentrate and harden and mature the kernel of his brain, to give tone and firmness and consistency to his thought. Then is the great harvest of the year, the harvest of thought." Winter is a time of mental harvest when thoughts are ripe for gleaning.

The setting as well as the climactic conditions affected Thoreau's ability to think. The following *Journal* entry illustrates how walking by a river influenced his mental sauntering: "What a difference it makes whether I spend my four hours' nooning between the hills by yonder roadside, or on the brink of this fair river, within a quarter of a mile of that! Here the earth is fluid to my thought, the sky is reflected from beneath, and around yonder cape is the highway to other continents. . . . There my thoughts were confined and trivial, and I hid myself from the gaze of travellers. Here they are expanded and elevated, and I am charmed by the beautiful river-reach."

Mountains could, like rivers, have their own special effect by raising Thoreau's thoughts above the trivial. His *Journal* account of a climb up Mount Monadnock describes how the higher altitude of the mountain and the uneven terrain "suggested so many thoughts" and affected him so that he "no longer thought and reasoned as in the plain." Concerning a different hike, Thoreau recorded: "It is worth the while to see the mountains in the horizon once a day. I have thus seen some earth which corresponds to my least earthly and trivial, to my most heavenward-looking, thoughts. . . . They are the natural *temples,* elevated brows, of the earth, looking at which, the thoughts of the beholder are naturally elevated and sublimed,—etherealized."

Any aspect of the external landscape affected Thoreau within. In "A Walk to Wachusett" he reveals how even a dusty road could influence his thinking processes: "At length, we plodded along the dusty roads, our thoughts became as dusty as they; all thought indeed stopped, thinking broke down, or proceeded only passively in a sort of rhythmical cadence of the confused material of thought." Something as simple as moonlight could have a far more beneficial effect, intellectually lighting the walker within even as the moon beams struck the landscape around him: "It must be allowed that the light of the moon [is] sufficient . . . for the pensive walker. . . . The poet who walks by moonlight is conscious of a tide in his thought which is to be referred to lunar influence" ("Night and Moonlight").

The process of internalization could be initiated by any external feature. Whether it was smooth water and the humming of mosquitoes—"My thoughts are driven inward, even as clouds and trees are reflected in the still, smooth water. There is an inwardness even in the mosquitoes's hum, while I am picking blueberries in the dank wood" (*Journal*); or the ripeness of an October day—"I am riper for thought, too" (*Journal*), Thoreau found himself being influenced by the external landscape to explore his own inner landscape.

The relationship between the walker and the environment is dynamic. In his *Journal* Thoreau comments that "the scenery, when it is truly seen, reacts on the life of the seer," and he compares himself to a bee out to "extract its honey from the flower of the world. That is my everyday business. . . . With what honeyed thought any experience yields me I take a bee line to my cell." He concludes

116

that "by the dawning or radiance of beauty are we advertised where is the honey and the fruit of thought, of discourse, and of action." Thoreau's ideas reflect Emerson's proposition that the beauty in the world has "a relation to thought. . . . The beauty of nature re-forms itself in the mind, and not for barren contemplation, but for new creation." This was Thoreau's goal—to allow the beauty of the external landscape to affect his mind and transform his inner world.

Walking, however, did more than put Thoreau's body in touch with his mind and foster the cooperation of these two aspects of his being. Walking also connected his body and mind with his soul, ultimately making possible the spiritual uplifting of his inner world. Thoreau was as aware of the importance of cooperation between body and soul as between body and mind. In his *Journal* (Princeton) he writes: "Good for the body is the work of the body, and good for the soul the work of the soul, and good for either the work of the other—let them not call hard names, nor know a divided interest."

Thoreau firmly believed in the integral connection between the body and the soul: "The great art of life is how to turn the surplus life of the soul into life for the body,— that so the life be not a failure."

Uniting body, mind, and soul was a difficult but important process: "To make a perfect man—the Soul must be much like the body not too unearthly & the body like the soul. The one must not deny & oppress the other" (*Journal* [Princeton]). Thoreau's walks involved a delicate balance between physical activity, which met the needs of the body; mental activity, which met the needs of the mind or reason; and spiritual activity, which met the needs of the soul. Maintaining this balance was challenging but rewarding for Thoreau, as this *Journal* (Princeton) musing reveals: "I cannot walk conveniently and pleasantly but when I hold myself far off in the horizon—and the soul dilutes the body and makes it passable—My soul and body have tottered along together of late tripping and hindering oneanother [sic] like unpractised Siamese twins—They two should walk as one that no obstacle may be nearer than the firmament."

Walking Thoreau-style involves letting each part—body, mind, and soul—carry out its natural function without interfering with each other. This was the ideal that he aimed at in his sauntering experience: "How wholesome are the natural laws to contemplate. . . . Only let us not interfere. Let the soul withdraw into the chambers of the heart—let the mind reside steadily in the labyrinth of the brain, and not interfere with hands or feet more than with other parts of nature."

So interconnected was Thoreau's experience that he viewed physical and emotional health as dependent upon spiritual health and measured his walking experience by the health he enjoyed at the time of the walk. The health of his body, mind, and soul were dependent on walking in nature, where nature's restorative influences could affect the saunterer without interference. The physical act of walking combines with the rejuvenating powers of the environment to ensure the walker's physical, emotional, and spiritual well-being: "In society you will not find health but in nature—You must converse much with the field and woods if you would imbibe such health into your mind and spirit as you covet for your body. . . . Without that our feet at least stood in the midst of nature all our faces would be pale and livid" (*Journal* [Princeton]).

When in nature, the very action of walking encourages a corresponding marching of the saunterer's soul, bringing the walker inspiration and moral courage: "To the sensitive soul, the universe has its own fixed measure, which is its measure also, and as a regular pulse is insepa-rable from a healthy body, so is its healthiness dependent on the regularity of its rythm [sic], and seeks to express its sympathy by a correspondent movement of the limbs. When the body marches to the measure of the soul, then is true courage and invincible strength" (*Journal* [Princeton]).

Thoreau used his walking experience as a way to measure his own vital signs. The spirit of his walks corresponded with his physical, emotional, and spiritual health. In his *Journal* he declares: "Measure your health by your sympathy with morning and spring. If there is no response in you to the awakening of nature,—if the prospect of an early morning walk does not banish sleep, . . . know that the morning and spring of your life are past. Thus you may feel your pulse."

When Thoreau wrote to his friends, he often described his own health in terms of his current walking ability. Such was the case when he wrote Daniel Ricketson in 1857 and noted that there were few signs of spring in himself, although the April weather outside would normally have evoked such. He summarized his condition with this statement: "I am decent for steady pace but not yet for a race" (*Correspondence*). Canby observes that poor health affected Thoreau most when it came to his walking experience: "For Thoreau, of course, weakness would be most resented in those sturdy pistons that had to propel him over so many miles of wood and pasture walking. If he could not count on his legs, he was a sad man indeed."

The life of the body and the mind were very important to Thoreau, and, from his transcendentalist viewpoint, inseparably linked with the life of the soul, but he most valued the life of the soul. His walks were ultimately spiritual pilgrimages to the god he found in nature and in himself; they linked him with the divine. Thoreau claimed, "My profession is to be always on the alert to find God in nature, to know his lurking-places, to attend all the oratorios, the operas, in nature."

At the heart of Thoreau's saunterings as spiritual pilgrimage was the transcendental belief in the divinity of man: "I think that we are not commonly aware that man is our contemporary,—that in this strange, outlandish world, so barren, so prosaic, fit not to live in but merely to pass through, that even here so divine a creature as man does actually live. Man, the crowning fact, the god we know." Transcendentalists believed that man has divinity within himself even as nature is infused with the divine; the transcendental oversoul permeates everything and unites it in a spiritual bond. When man walks in nature, divinity is placed within the context of divinity; spiritual connects with spiritual: "I think that the existence of man in nature is the divinest and most startling of all facts." Emerson made clear that man's soul finds its counterpart in nature—"He shall see that nature is the opposite of the soul, answering to it part for part. One is seal and one is print" ("The American Scholar"). Because of the openness of the walking experience, nothing interfered with this spiritual correspondence between man and nature.

In his essay "Walking" Thoreau proclaims the importance of the spiritual nature of the walking experience: "They who never go to the Holy Land in their walks, as they pretend, are indeed mere idlers and vagabonds; but they who do go there are saunterers in the good sense, such as I mean. . . . For every walk is a sort of crusade, preached by some Peter the Hermit in us, to go forth and reconquer this Holy Land from the hands of the Infidels."

His *Journal* makes clear that he viewed his walks as sanctioned by God—"I have a charter, though it be from Heaven alone, to travel the course I do. . . . It is by the grace of God . . ."; and when he walked in nature, it gave him a spiritual freedom that he could not find in the city. In a letter to Isaiah Williams, who had described to Thoreau how transcendentalism had freed him from what he felt were the shackles of Christianity, Thoreau wrote: "I think I can sympathize with your sense of greater freedom. . . . As for creeds and doctrines we are suddenly grown rustic—and from walking in streets and squares—walk broadly in the fields—as if a man were wise enough not to sit in a draft, and get an ague, but moved buoyantly in the breeze."

One reason why walking spiritually liberated Thoreau is that it requires the saunterer to maintain an upright position, with the head pointed toward heaven; the very posture of the walker suggests his spiritual transcendence. Thoreau felt that an upright position drew the walker toward heavenly things and away from the mundane matters of the feet. This was very important to him, as a letter he wrote to H. G. O. Blake indicates: "What a pity if we do not live this short time according to the laws of the long time,—the eternal laws! Let us see that we stand erect here, and do not lie along by our whole length in the dirt. . . . The laws of earth are for the feet, or inferior man; the laws of heaven are for the head, or superior man."

Thoreau's emphasis on remaining upright—"Cultivate the habit of early rising. It is unwise to keep the head long on a level with the feet" (*Journal*)—was shared by Emerson, who stated in "Self-Reliance": "He who knows that power is inborn, that he is weak because he has looked for good out of him and elsewhere, and, so perceiving, throws himself unhesitatingly on his thought, instantly rights himself, stands in the erect position, commands his limbs, works miracles; just as a man who stands on his feet is stronger than a man who stands on his head."

Walking in an upright position was in itself an act of worship for Thoreau. He associated walking with spiritual growth and sleeping or resting with apathy or spiritual decline. In *The Maine Woods* he watched how his Christian Indian guide "spent his Sunday." He was unimpressed by the Indian's spiritual and physical lethargy. While the Indian kept Sunday holy by physically resting, Thoreau remained as active as ever, sauntering about the local landscape. Thoreau's religion was active, not passive, and walking perfectly suited it. Every day was a holy day for Thoreau, because every day presented the opportunity for a spiritual pilgrimage in nature. Once when Thoreau was reprimanded by a minister for walking on Sunday, he replied that he would go to church instead of walking if he thought he might "hear a true word spoken on that or any other day" (*A Week*). Thoreau felt that the only true words he might hear would be spoken in nature and not from a church pulpit, and to hear these words, he would need to walk in nature, not sit passively in a pew.

Thoreau was firm in his commitment to walk on Sunday instead of attend church. As a child he was required on Sundays to be inactive and to observe nature passively from his room. This made him crave activity all the more. Thus, for as long as he was physically able to walk, he sauntered every Sunday, worshiping his God in his own way. The only request made by his sweetheart, Ellen Sewall, which Thoreau denied, was her desire that he attend church with her. Walking outdoors was his form of worship he informed her. When Thoreau was queried by an Indian guide about what he did on Sundays, he replied that he often spent Sunday morning reading and "went to walk in the afternoon." The Indian's response— "Er, that is ver bad" (*The Maine Woods*)—represents the sentiments of Ellen Sewall and most people in Thoreau's day. His spiritual saunters were not popular, but this did not bother Thoreau; he consistently took his walks, Sunday or not, seeking the spiritual blessings they provided him.

At times Thoreau wondered if others experienced nature in the same way that he did, if they worshiped in a similar manner, but his experience taught him that his sauntering pilgrimages set him apart from his contemporaries: "When I am outside, on the outskirts of the town, enjoying the still majesty of the moor, I am wont to think that all men are aware of this miracle, that they too are silently worshipping this manifestation of divinity elsewhere. But when I go into the house I am undeceived; they are absorbed in checkers or chess or novel, though they may have been advertised of the brightness through the shutters" (*Journal*).

As with the relationship between walking and thinking, Thoreau's spiritual sauntering involved drawing correspondences between the observable phenomena of the landscape and something dormant within himself, in this case spiritual truths. Typical is this *Journal* account of his discovery of a particular flower, the johnswort, during an afternoon walk: "It affected me, this tender dome-like bud, within the bosom of the earth, like a temple upon the earth, resounding with the worship of votaries. Me thought I saw the flamens in yellow robes within it. The crowfoot buds—and how many beside!—lie unexpanded just beneath the surface. May I lead my life the following year as innocently as they! May it be as fair and smell as sweet! I anticipate nature. Destined to become a fair yellow flower above the surface to delight the eyes of children and its Maker. It offered to my mind a little temple into which to enter and worship."

Any natural fact could inspire spiritual faith. When Thoreau observed green ferns surviving into October, he concluded in his *Journal:* "Even in them I feel an argument for immortality. Death is so far from being universal. The same destroyer does not destroy all. How valuable they are . . . for cheerfulness." Seeing the mark left on a tree by a lightning bolt projected Thoreau into a state of reverence: "I was impressed with awe on looking up and seeing that broad, distinct spiral mark . . . mark of an invisible and intangible power, a thunderbolt, mark where a terrific and resistless bolt came down from heaven, out of the harmless sky. . . . It seemed such a sacred spot." Even noting snowflakes during a winter saunter connected Thoreau with a sense of the divine: "A divinity must have stirred within them before the crystals did thus shoot and set." To sense the divine influence in a snowflake may not seem that surprising, but to glean spiritual nutriment out of plain rocks demonstrates how easily Thoreau's observation of external phenomena was converted to spiritual insights and internal transformations. In his *Journal* he records his excitement at discovering a place that was especially wild and rugged, marked primarily by rocks: "I would fain improve every opportunity to wonder and worship, as a sunflower welcomes the light. The more thrilling, wonderful, divine objects I behold in a day, the more expanded and immortal I become. If a stone appeals to me and elevates me, tells me how many miles I have come, how many remain to travel,—and the more, the better,—reveals the future to me in some measure, it is a matter of private rejoicing. If it did the same service to all, it might well be a matter of public rejoicing."

When Thoreau walked, he often responded to nature by analogy, drawing on the similarities between what he observed and his own experience. During one November hike, Thoreau compared the sun's warming of the landscape with the warmth of the Creator toward man. When walking at night, he concluded, "Our spiritual side takes a more distinct form, like our shadow which we see accompanying us." When looking for signs of life in a sand bank during a March ramble, he philosophized: "The eternity which I detect in Nature I predicate of myself also. How many springs I have had this same experience! I am encouraged, for I recognize this steady persistency and recovery of Nature as a quality of myself." Oak leaves, dying in the fall, seemed like "saints or innocent and beneficent beings." "How spiritual" they appeared to Thoreau, who sensed their analogous relationship to "the perseverance of the saints."

The landscape easily evokes such analogies from a walker like Thoreau because walking makes possible the kind of close observation and reflective thinking that make such comparisons possible. Only walking provides the traveler with the leisure and vantage point to ensure the direct flow of spiritual insight from observable phenomena to the walker. Only walking makes possible the natural conversion of the external to the internal without interference or distraction.

Just as sensual encounters with the landscape, made possible by walking, trigger new worlds of thought, so sense stimuli evoke spiritual insights and experiences. Sensual contact with nature is simply a first and necessary step for a walker like Thoreau that leads to intellectual and spiritual internalization of the landscape. One can readily observe in his writings how this transfer from sensual to spiritual occurred during Thoreau's walks. For example, Thoreau records his response to hearing the echoes of his own voice during a woodland saunter. Enchanted, he remarks that it would be interesting to travel about the country looking for places where one's echo could be heard—"prophetic places" suited to the "sacred ears of Nature." The most simple sounds could launch Thoreau into a spiritual reverie. During one May walk, when he listened to the creak of crickets, he felt that their chirps suggested "lateness, but only as we come to a knowledge of eternity after some acquaintance with time." He comments that their "chant" had an "eternal" quality to it, and concludes that "it is heaven where they are. . . ." These cricket songs affected him as "a glorifying of God and enjoying him forever." Even the sound of the wind playing against the telegraph wires transformed his inner state, converting his ramble into an uplifting transcendental experience.

When, in 1852, Thoreau sauntered through the Concord countryside, depressed by what he had seen and heard the previous day concerning a powder-mill explosion, the sound of these wires raised his spirits and tuned him to the spiritual: "This wire is my redeemer. It always brings a special and a general message to me from the Highest. Day before yesterday I looked at the mangled and blackened bodies of men which had been blown up by powder, and felt that the lives of men were not innocent, and that there was an avenging power in nature. Today I hear this immortal melody, while the west wind is blowing balmily on my cheek, and methinks a roseate sunset is preparing. Are there not two powers?"

Any combination of sense appeals, such as sight and hearing, produced similar spiritual states: "In the sunshine and the crowing of cocks I feel an illimitable holiness, which makes me bless God and myself. The warm sun casts his incessant gift at my feet as I walk along— unfolding his yellow worlds" (Princeton). In a *Journal* record of a walk taken right after an ice storm Thoreau converts a sense appeal into a spiritual application: "The bells are particularly sweet this morning. . . . How much more religion in their sound, than they ever call men together to! Men obey their call and go to the stove-warmed church, though God exhibits himself to the walker in a frosted bush to-day, as much as in a burning one to Moses of old." Thoreau's senses provided nature with direct access to not only his body and mind, but also his soul.

The general features and conditions of the landscape affected Thoreau's spiritual state as much as did the specific phenomena that he observed. This was especially evident during Thoreau's mountain walks. The higher altitudes and grander perspectives drew his thoughts heavenward. Like John Bunyan's pilgrim, Thoreau ascended the hills and mountains surrounding Concord with a spiritual destination in sight—the actual raised ascent paralleled a spiritual one. When climbing a mountain in the summer of 1844, Thoreau noted, "It seemed a very fit rout for the pilgrim to enter upon who is climbing to the gates of heaven" (Princeton).

Mountains are the saunterer's touchstones between earth and heaven. They are the physical intermediary between the land of the material and the land of the spiritual, as this *Journal* entry illustrates: "The value of the mountains in the horizon,—would not that be a good theme for a lecture? The text for a discourse on real values, and permanent; a sermon on the mount. They are stepping-stones to heaven,—as the rider has a horse-block at his gate,—by which to mount when we would commence our pilgrimage to heaven."

Some of Thoreau's walks were taken for the express purpose of seeing distant mountains. Their view inspired him and rewarded him for the trouble of his journey: "I go to Flint's Pond for the sake of the mountain view from the hill beyond, looking over Concord. . . . They are the natural *temples*, elevated brows, of the earth, looking at which, the thoughts of the beholder are naturally elevated and sublimed,—etherealized. I wish to see the earth through the medium of much air or heaven, for there is no paint like the air. Mountains thus seen are worthy of worship."

Climbing a mountain, rather than merely observing it from a distance, provided Thoreau with more direct spiritual experiences, enabling him to better understand his body and soul. In a letter to H. G. O. Blake he commented that he felt "the same awe when on [mountain] summits that many do on entering a church." He believed that "you must ascend a mountain to learn your relation to matter, and so to your own body, for it is at home there, though you are not. It might have been composed there, and will have no farther to go to return to dust there, than in your garden; but your spirit inevitably comes away, and brings your body with it, if it lives."

In a different letter to Blake, Thoreau's recollection of a mountain walk reveals the spiritual significance of the mountain setting to the walker: "I remember that walk to Asnebumskit very well;—a fit place to go on a Sunday, one of the true temples of the earth. A temple you know was anciently 'an open place without a roof,' whose walls served merely to shut out the world, and direct the mind toward heaven; but a modern *meeting house* shuts out the heavens, while it crowds the world into still closer quarters. Best of all is it when as on a Mt. top you have for all walls your own elevations and deeps of surrounding ether."

Of course, more than mountainous environments compelled Thoreau to spiritually saunter while he walked from day to day. In winter, walking in the snow not only revealed to him tracks of men and animals, but also moral qualities which he wished to apply to his own life: "Why do the vast snow plains give us pleasure, the twilight of the bent and half-buried woods? Is not all there consonant with virtue, justice, purity, courage, magnanimity? Are we not cheered by the sight? And does not all this amount to the track of a higher life than the otter's, a life which has not gone by and left a footprint merely, but is there with its beauty, its music, its perfume, its sweetness, to exhilarate and recreate us? . . . The great game for mighty hunters as soon as the first snow falls is Purity" (*Journal*).

The purity of snow suggested to Thoreau a divine quality within himself, as was the case when he hiked across a frozen Walden Pond one February day and noted: "I go across Walden. My shadow is very blue. It is especially blue when there is a bright sunlight on pure white snow. It suggests that there may be something divine, something celestial in me."

Although not as lofty as mountains, nor as pure as snowy fields, swamps and meadows offered Thoreau their own form of spiritual insight and experience. When he walked, his church or temple was the place where he was at the time, including swamps. He observed, "If there were Druids whose temples were the oak groves, my temple is the swamp."

Walking through a meadow could revive a sense of the sacredness and eternity of life, a discovery Thoreau made at Walden: "Ah! I have penetrated to those meadows on the morning of many a first spring day, jumping from hummock to hummock, from willow root to willow root, when the wild river valley and the woods were bathed in so pure and bright a light as would have waked the dead, if they had been slumbering in their graves, as some suppose. There needs no stronger proof of immortality. All things must live in such a light. O Death, where was thy sting? O Grave, where was thy victory, then?"

Whatever the environment or conditions, Thoreau's walks yielded spiritual experiences and insights that affected his inner life. The act of walking that involved the cooperation of body, mind, and soul, and the relationship between specific natural phenomena, the general environment, and the walker himself directed Thoreau from his sensual awareness of the physical, external world to the spiritual world beneath nature's surface and within himself.

In much the same way, these same dynamics sensually tied him to the landscape, providing him with physical challenges and heroic adventures, and triggering his thoughts as he explored his own internal landscape. At each level—physical, emotional, mental, and spiritual—walking made possible experiences that resulted from the harmonious cooperation of the saunterer's body, mind, and soul as they interacted with the environment.

Thoreau's saunterings followed the general transcendental pattern of converting from the external to the internal. They involved a very important internalization process that enabled him, after first making contact with nature and studying it, to explore new worlds within himself—to probe his own emotions, thoughts, and spiritual dimensions as he sought correspondences between the external landscape and his own private world. This process marked the essence of his walking experience.

4

THE ESSENTIAL SELF

In a Stephen Crane poem written over thirty years after Thoreau's death, the protagonist proclaims to the universe: "Sir, I exist!" The universe's reply—"The fact has not created in me/A sense of obligation"—reveals the stark alienation between nature and the self, which exists in a naturalistic world. Had Thoreau composed this poem, the universe might well have stated: "The fact creates in me every obligation to fulfill your essential self."

In Thoreau's world, self was all, and sauntering—more than just a way to transform experience into thoughts and feelings—provided him with the opportunity to assert and to fulfill his essential self. Rambling separated Thoreau from society and those influences that he felt corrupted his true being. At the same time it met his social needs and made him a better member of society. Unlike T. S. Eliot's Prufrock, who, trapped and surrounded by a threatening society, found his life measured in coffee spoons, Thoreau used walking to escape the restrictions of society; his life was measured, not in coffee spoons, but in footsteps that took him away from the drawing-room world of trivial chatter that so intimidated Prufrock.

The roads and paths that led Thoreau away from society when he sauntered reveal a great deal about the relationship between his walking experience and his need to assert and fulfill himself. The roads that Thoreau chose to follow matched the course of his own thinking.

Thoreau sought those roads and paths that would remove him from all visible signs of civilization, and, in doing so, place him in the fancy-free environment that his essential self required. The more he walked away from the taints of society, the freer he was to engage in internal sauntering, to follow the paths that led to the self: "Now I yearn for one of those old, meandering, dry, uninhabited roads, which lead away from towns, . . . along which you may travel like a pilgrim, going nowhither; where travellers are not too often to be met; where my spirit is free; where the walls and fences are not cared for; where your head is more in heaven than your feet are on earth . . . ; There I can walk, and recover the lost child that I am without any ringing of a bell; . . . There I have freedom in my thought, and in my soul am free. I must be fancy-free." As these reflections indicate, isolated roads that offered few distractions helped Thoreau confront his essential self.

Roads such as the one Thoreau describes, however, are difficult for the saunterer to find, since most roads lead toward, not away from, civilization, and, consequently, confront the walker with numerous distractions. Still, Thoreau maintains in "Walking" that there are at least "one or two such roads in every town." In "Walking" Thoreau cites a poem, "The Old Marlborough Road," which describes the ideal road for a saunterer like himself who wishes to escape the influences of the society:

> When the spring stirs my blood
> With the instinct to travel,
> I can get enough gravel
> On the Old Marlborough Road.
> Nobody repairs it,
> For nobody wears it;

It is a living way,
As the Christians say.
Not many there be
Who enter therein,
Only the guest of the
Irishman Quin.
What is it, what is it,
But a direction out there,
And the bare possibility
Of going somewhere?

Thoreau needed roads like the Marlborough Road, which release the walker from a sense of destination and responsibility, because they purged him from the corrupting influences of the city.

Unlike the Marlborough Road, most roads provide the traveler with a goal or destination and a connection with society. Thoreau often found his walking experience undermined when he walked on a road that led to a town or city. Such a road drew not only his body but his thoughts toward civilization and away from the solitude of nature, which was so essential to his emotional, spiritual, and physical well-being. Under these circumstances, Thoreau's walking experience became mechanical and unrewarding. "When you get into the road, though far from the town, and feel the sand under your feet, it is as if you had reached your own gravel walk. You no longer hear the whip-poor-will, nor regard your shadow, for here you expect a fellow-traveler. You catch yourself walking merely. The road leads your steps and thoughts alike to town. You see only the path, and your thoughts wander from the objects which are presented to your senses. You are no longer in place. It is like conformity,—walking in the ways of men." Hiking a road that presented too many reminders of society seriously hampered Thoreau's exploration of the self.

Although Thoreau's spirit was seldom rejuvenated when he walked on a road toward town, when the road carried him away from civilization, he experienced a welcome sense of release and freedom: "I go along the settled road, where the houses are interspersed with woods, in an unaccountably desponding mood, but when I come out upon a bare and solitary heath am at once exhilarated. This is a common experience in my travelling. I plod along, thinking what a miserable world this is and what miserable fellows we that inhabit it, wondering what it is tempts men to live in it; but anon I leave the towns behind and am lost in some boundless heath, and life becomes gradually more tolerable, if not even glorious." Thoreau's internal sauntering often began at that point where the road's reminders of civilization left off and the open, inviting world of nature began.

Unlike the world of nature, which rejuvenated Thoreau's self, the artificial world of man drained his spirit. This is one reason why his walks were so important to him. While in the city, he found himself stifled. Only in a natural environment could Thoreau revive the self that the city suffocated. So extreme was his aversion to a city environment that he did all that he could to avoid even walking through a city: "I do not love to go through a village street any more than a cottage yard. I feel that I am there only by sufferance; but I love to go by the villages by my own road, seeing them from one side, as I do theoretically. When I go through a village, my legs ache at the prospect of the hard graveled walk. I go by the tavern with its porch full of gazers, and meet a miss taking a walk or the doctor in his sulky, and for half an hour I feel as strange as if I were in a town in China; but soon I am at home in the wide world again, and my feet rebound from the yielding turf."

The road that offered a pathway to the self was the one that led away from the city into "the wide world." The road that led to the city offered a path, not for the self alone, but for society in general, and this could only mean one thing to a staunch transcendentalist like Thoreau—conformity. Thoreau viewed main-traveled roads as symbols of the conformity that the men who traveled them exhibited in their own lives. The reluctance of the townspeople to leave the road and break free in their travels signaled their conformity in all areas of life. It took only a snow cover to reveal such a state: "Though the snow was not deep, I noticed that an unbroken snow-crust stretched around Fitchburg, and its several thousand inhabitants had been confined so long to the narrow streets, some of them a track only six feet wide. Hardly one individual had anywhere departed from this narrow walk and struck out into the surrounding fields and hills. If I had had my cowhide boots, I should not have confined myself to those narrow limits, but have climbed some of the hills. It is surprising to go into a New England town in midwinter and find its five thousand inhabitants all living thus on the limits, confined at most to their narrow moose-yard in the snow."

For Thoreau, the roads and paths a man walked revealed the conformity or nonconformity of his own life: "The other afternoon I met Sam H—— walking on the railroad between the depot and the back road. It was something quite novel to see him there, though the railroad there is only a short thoroughfare to the public road. It then occurred to me that I had never met Mr. H. on the railroad, though he walks every day, and moreover that it would be quite impossible for him to walk on the railroad, such a formalist as he is, such strait-jackets as we weave for ourselves. He could do nothing that was not sanctioned by the longest use of men, and as men had voted in all their assemblies from the first to travel on the public way, he would confine himself to that. . . . I stood to see what he would do. He turned off the rails directly on to the back road and pursued his walk. A passing train will never meet him on the railroad causeway. How much of the life of certain men goes to sustain, to make respected, the institutions of society."

Unlike the conformist traveler described in this *Journal* account, Thoreau frequently walked the railroad and any other pathway that offered an escape from the restrictions of society. He often viewed roads as obstacles to successful walks, and he left their restricting courses whenever he had the opportunity to walk in paths of his own making. Even as Robert Frost asserted that there is something that does not love a wall, Thoreau maintained that there is something within the walker that does not love a public road. Thoreau frequently left the road to seek the healing powers of the countryside and to avoid anything, even the sound of his own footsteps, which might distract him from the unadulterated contact with nature that his walks made possible. Ralph Waldo Emerson wrote: "He had many elegances of his own, whilst he scoffed at conventional elegance. Thus, he could not bear to hear the sound of his own steps, the grit of gravel; and therefore never willingly walked in the road, but in the grass, on mountains and in woods" ("Thoreau").

In his *Journal* Thoreau celebrates how leaving the road and charting his own course rejuvenated him: "I felt my spirits rise when I had got off the road into the open fields, and the sky had a new appearance. I stepped along more buoyantly. . . . Before I walked in the ruts of travel; now I adventured."

Because of this sense of personal freedom that Thoreau experienced when he, and not the road, dictated the course of his saunterings, he considered the paths that his good genius directed him to take during his walks superior to the public roads of his day. Certainly his rambles through the countryside were better than wagon travel or any other conventional travel mode that would be confined to a road or track: "Flag Hill is about eight miles *by the road* from Concord. We went much further, going and returning both; but by how much nobler road! Suppose you were to ride to Boxboro, what then? You pass a few teams with their dust, drive through many farmers' barn-yards, between two walls, see where Squire Tuttle lives and barrels his apples, bait your horse at White's Tavern, and so return, with your hands smelling of greasy leather and horsehair and the squeak of a chaise body in your ears, with no new flower nor agreeable experience. But, going as we did, before you got to Boxboro line, you often went much further, many times ascended New Hampshire hills, taking the noble road from hill to hill, across swamps and valleys, not regarding political courses and boundaries, many times far west in your thought. It is a journey of a day and a picture of human life."

Once Thoreau left the road during his walks, he often went across lots, identifying more with the animals who traveled the same way than with the men who remained on the road: "I go across lots like a hunting dog. With what tireless energy and abandonment they dash through the brush and up the sides of hills! I meet two white foxhounds, led by an old red one. . . . They are not tied to paths."

Thoreau traversed the lots of Concord farmers in such private fashion that they were seldom aware of how frequently he walked through their property. In "The Succession of Forest Trees" he confided to his neighbors: "Moreover, taking a surveyor's and a naturalist's liberty, I have been in the habit of going across your lots much oftener than is usual, as many of you, perhaps to your sorrow, are aware. Yet many of you, to my relief, have seemed not to be aware of it; and, when I came across you in some out-of-the-way nook of your farms, have inquired, with an air of surprise, if I were not lost, since you had never seen me in that part of the town or county before; when, if the truth were known . . . , I might with more propriety have inquired if *you* were not lost, since I had never seen *you* there before. I have several times shown the proprietor the shortest way out of his wood-lot."

Like the men Thoreau addresses in this passage, Thoreau's townsmen were often unaware of his private, across-lots excursions, assuming that his walks were confined to public roads: "Getting over the wall near Sam Barrett's the other day, I had gone a few rods in the road when I met Prescott Barrett, who observed, 'Well, you take a walk round the square sometimes.' So little does he know of my habits. I go across lots over his grounds every three or four weeks, but I do not know that I ever walked round the square in my life."

One reason why many of his contemporaries did not realize how often Thoreau walked through their property in his quest to escape the limitations of the roads is that when sauntering across lots, Thoreau did all that he could to avoid seeing or being seen by people. The more private and isolated his walks, the more they refreshed his spirit and strengthened him to return to face the society that he had left. Thoreau went so far as to position himself when passing a house so that a tree would intervene between himself and the windows of a house, and he walked during inclement weather in order to enjoy the privacy such conditions offered him by shielding him from his contemporaries who remained inside. So strong was his desire to remove himself from any taint of civilization that Thoreau felt much more comfortable traversing natural ground than cultivated fields—"I love to get out of cultivated fields where I walk on an imported sod, on English grass, and walk in the fine sedge of woodland hollows, on an American sward. In the former case my thoughts are heavy and lumpish, as if I fed on turnips. In the other I nibble groundnuts."

Thoreau's *Journal* refers frequently to his desire to isolate himself from houses and cultivated fields that served as symbols of the society from which his walks were designed to liberate him. In October 2, 1859, Thoreau noted: "How much pleasanter to go along the edge of the woods, through the field in the rear of the farmhouse, whence you see only its gray roof and its haystacks, than to keep by its door! This we think as we return behind Martial Miles's." A June 1853 entry states: "But I travel chiefly in the fields or pastures parallel with the road." He adds, "These are very agreeable pastures to me; no house in sight, no cultivation." Only a few days earlier, Thoreau had written, "The fields a walker loves best to strike into are bare, extended, rolling, bordered by copses, with brooks and meadows in sight . . . , where is no high grass nor grain nor cultivated ground nor houses near."

Footpaths offered Thoreau the isolation he desired. He sought "an open path which would suggest walking and adventuring on it, the going to some place strange and far away." A *Journal* note reveals his preference for a footpath: "I would fain travel by a footpath round the world. I do not ask the railroads of commerce, not even the cartpaths of the farmer. Pray, what other path would you have than a footpath? What else should wear a path? This is the track of man alone. What more suggestive to the pensive walker."

Old roads that appealed primarily to walkers because they were seldom traveled and were in poor repair also attracted Thoreau. He praises the virtues of one such road—the old Carlisle road: "Going along this old Carlisle road,—road for walkers, for berry-pickers, and no more worldly travellers; road for Melvin and Clark, not for the sheriff nor butcher nor the baker's jingling cart; road where all wild things and fruits abound, where there are countless rocks to jar those who venture there in wagons; which no jockey, no wheelwright in his right mind, drives over, no little spidery gigs and Flying Childers; road which leads to and through a great but not famous garden, zoological and botanical garden, at whose gate you never arrive."

The more open such a road was, the more open Thoreau's thinking could be. Thoreau's self required space. He did not like standing too close to people when conversing with them, and he could not tolerate the feeling of being hampered by physical barriers of any kind. One thing that Thoreau's walking experience reveals is how easily the physical elements of the landscape affected his thinking processes. Open space led to open thinking; confined space hampered his thinking. Thus Thoreau could tolerate no fences in his own life, and the same held true for the roads and paths that he sauntered along. Open roads and paths appealed to the openness that marked the breadth of his own life-style: "The road through the pitch pine woods beyond J. Hosmer's is very pleasant to me, curving under the pines, without a fence. . . . I love to see a sandy road like this carving through a pitch pine wood where the trees closely border it without fences, a great cart-path merely."

Along with openness and freedom, Thoreau required of a road or path, as he did of his own life, that there be wildness. This is what he found appealing about walking the railroad: "The railroad is perhaps our pleasantest and wildest road. It only makes deep cuts into and through the hills. On it are no houses nor foot-travellers. The travel on it does not disturb me. The woods are left to hang over it. Though straight, is wild in its accompaniments. All is raw edges."

Thoreau experienced this kind of openness and wildness when he hiked the more natural roadways provided by nature herself, such as a frozen river: "It is much easier and pleasanter to walk thus on the river . . . , and this road is so wide that you do not feel confined in it, and you never meet travellers with whom you have no sympathy."

In wintertime Thoreau found "three great highways" heading out from his door, three frozen river branches that offered him personal freedom in his walking experience: "Could any avenues be contrived more convenient? With this river I am not compelled to walk in the tracks of horses." As with the railroad, the river bordered the wildness of nature and offered the winter saunterer or skater a passage into nature unobtainable by any other path: "The river flows in the rear of the towns, and we see all things from a new and wilder side. The fields and gardens come down to it with a frankness, and freedom from pretension, which they do not wear on the highway. It is the outside and edge of the earth" ("A Winter Walk"). Thoreau's self responded to wildness as to space, and these natural, wild paths offered him some of the best opportunities for internal sauntering.

Walking in and of itself offered no panacea for Thoreau's mental and emotional health. As his experiences with roads and paths indicate, where and how he walked spelled the difference. His walks away from the city helped get society and politics out of his head and cleared his thinking for the internal sauntering that put him in touch with himself. Any other transportation form would have reminded him of civilization, but walking carried no such associations. Instead, it freed him from ties to others and to society in general, and it enabled him to maintain a very healthy sense of personal well-being.

The importance of Thoreau's walks away from civilization and their connection to his emotional health is recorded in his *Journal* entry for January 7, 1857. This particular description of his walking experience offers one of the most convincing portrayals of how significant his saunterings were to his personal well-being: "In the street and in society I am almost invariably cheap and dissipated, my life is unspeakably mean. No amount of gold or respectability would in the least redeem it,— dining with the Governor or a member of Congress!! But alone in distant woods or fields, in unpretending sprout-lands or pastures tracked by rabbits, even in a bleak and, to most, cheerless day, like this, when a villager would be thinking of his inn, I come to myself, I once more feel myself grandly related, and that cold and solitude are friends of mine. I suppose that this value, in my case, is equivalent to what others get by churchgoing and prayer. I come to my solitary woodland walk as the homesick go home." This passage clarifies that only by walking away from society could Thoreau dispel all thoughts of the artificial existence that he associated with the city, and, in doing so, "once more feel" himself.

Modern literary heroes like Stephen Dedalus and Leopold Bloom work out their identities while walking in the city, but Thoreau was a true romantic who needed to walk away from the city in order to affirm his identity. Thoreau viewed walking away from the city and into nature as a way to combat the ills of urbanization. In nature he found freedom from the constraints of institutionalization.

Concord gave Thoreau reason enough to distrust city life. During Thoreau's adult years, Concord experienced growing industrialization, commercialization, and materialism. Its increasingly sophisticated and materialistically-minded residents created pressures for conformity that seriously threatened Thoreau's independent nature.

Thoreau found it necessary to escape these undesirable influences of city life in order to affirm his own identity.

Every aspect of city life repelled him and threatened his personal search for fulfillment: "What is the village, city, State, nation, aye the civilized world, that it should concern a man so much?" he queried in his *Journal*, and then added: "I do not value any view of the universe into which man and the institutions of man enter very largely and absorb much of the attention. Man is but the place where I stand, and the prospect hence is infinite."

When Thoreau spent time at Staten Island, he confided to his friend, Emerson, his strong aversion to city life: "I don't like the city better, the more I see it, but worse. I am ashamed of my eyes that behold it. It is a thousand times meaner that I could have imagined. It will be something to hate,—that's the advantage it will be to me." So strong was this repulsion, that Thoreau even dreaded hikes into the city library to read books. As much as he enjoyed reading, the city environment suffocated him: "But if I would read their [naturalists] books I must go to the city,—so strange and repulsive both to them and to me,— and deal with men and institutions with whom I have no sympathy. When I have just been there on this errand, it seems too great a price to pay for access even to the works of Homer, or Chaucer, or Linnaeus."

A number of Thoreau's *Journal* entries record the contrast in his experience between city walking and country walking. One winter entry depicts certain drawbacks of city life that taint the walker's experience: "What a difference between life in the city and in the country at present,—between walking in Washington Street, threading your way between countless sledges and travellers, over the discolored snow, and crossing Walden Pond, a spotless field of snow surrounded by woods, whose intensely blue shadows and your own are the only objects. What a solemn silence reigns here!"

A summer entry focuses on the impurity of city life when contrasted with the purity of country life: "As I walk through these old deserted wild orchards, half pasture, half huckleberry-field, the air is filled with fragrance from I know not what source. How much purer and sweeter it must be than the atmosphere of the streets, rendered impure by the filth about our houses! It is quite offensive often when the air is heavy at night. The roses in the front yard do not atone for the sink and pigsty and cow-yard and jakes in the rear."

In every respect Thoreau viewed a city as morally corrupting and generally debilitating: "It is folly to attempt to educate children within a city; the first step must be to remove them out of it."

Only when he was completely free from the world of men could he truly find himself: "It is impossible for me to be interested in what interests men generally. Their pursuits and interests seem to me frivolous. When I am most myself and see the clearest, men are least to be seen."

For Thoreau, walking away from the city was not as automatic as it might seem. In "Walking" he reveals how his walks were failures unless he removed the city from his mind as well as from his body: "Of course it is of no use to direct our steps to the woods, if they do not carry us thither. I am alarmed when it happens that I have walked a mile into the woods bodily, without getting there in spirit. In my afternoon walk I would fain forget all my morning occupations and my obligations to society. But it sometimes happens that I cannot easily shake off the village. The thought of some work will run in my head and I am not where my body is,—I am out of my senses. In my walks I would fain return to my senses. What business have I in the woods, if I am thinking of something out of the woods?"

The effort to forsake the city and saunter into nature called for the united efforts of body, soul, and mind. Away from the city, the body relaxed, but this availed little if the mind failed to escape the tensions of city life. Thoreau comments on how thoughts of societal concerns ruined his walks: "We walk to lakes to see our serenity reflected in them. When we are not serene, we go not to them. Who can be serene in a country where both rulers and ruled are without principle? The remembrance of the baseness of politicians spoils my walks."

It was especially difficult for Thoreau to keep his thinking untainted when he returned from his walks to the city: "Though you may have sauntered near to heaven's gate, when at length you return toward the village you give up the enterprise a little, and you begin to fall into the old ruts of thought, like a regular roadster. . . . Your thoughts turn toward night and the evening mail and become begrimed with dust."

Thoreau's walks away from the city and into nature were necessary for his well-being. The world of man burdened his spirit, but nature offered a world solely for the self: "I love Nature partly *because* she is not man, but a retreat from him. None of his institutions control or pervade her. There a different kind of right prevails. In her midst I can be glad with an entire gladness. If this world were all man, I could not stretch myself, I should lose all hope. He is constraint, she is freedom to me. He makes me wish for another world. She makes me content with this."

The magnetic pull of nature is a recurrent theme in Thoreau's *Journal*. In one typical entry, he confesses: "In the society of many men, or in the midst of what is called success, I find my life of no account, and my spirits rapidly fall. . . . But when I have only a rustling oak leaf, or the faint metallic cheep of a tree sparrow, for variety in my winter walk, my life becomes continent and sweet as the kernel of a nut."

Another *Journal* entry records a similar sentiment: "While most keep to their parlor fires this cold and blustering

Thanksgiving afternoon, and think with compassion of those abroad, I find the sunny south side of this swamp as warm as their parlors, and warmer to my spirit."

Thoreau's sanity was based, not on the affairs of men, but the affairs of nature. Walking in nature launched him into a world far more fulfilling than the superficial world of human society, a point Thoreau makes in "Life Without Principle": "All summer, and far into the autumn, perchance, you unconsciously went by the newspapers and the news, and now you find it was because the morning and the evening were full of news to you. Your walks were full of incidents. You attended, not to the affairs of Europe, but to your own affairs in Massachusetts fields. . . . Really to see the sun rise or go down every day, so to relate ourselves to a universal fact, would preserve us sane forever."

In *Cape Cod* Thoreau observes: "I was glad to have got out of the towns, where I am wont to feel unspeakably mean and disgraced,—to have left behind me for a season the bar-rooms of Massachusetts, where the full-grown are not weaned from savage and filthy habits,—still sucking a cigar. My spirits rose in proportion to the outward dreariness. The towns need to be ventilated."

One irony of Thoreau's walking experience is that no matter how much his walks in nature rejuvenated and affirmed him, they also led him back to the city and the society from which he wished to escape. The circular nature of Thoreau's walks, from city to nature and back to city again, reveals a deep inner tension that he experienced within himself. He walked away from the city because he felt an irresistible pull to nature. "Hope and the future for me are not in lawns and cultivated fields, not in towns and cities, but in the impervious and quaking swamps," Thoreau announced in "Walking." Later in the same essay he asserted: "When I would recreate my-

self, I seek the darkest wood, the thickest and most inter-
minable and, to the citizen, most dismal, swamp. . . .
A town is saved, not more by the righteous men in it than
by the woods and swamps that surround it."

What is interesting, but not surprising, is that Thoreau
also felt a pull, be it a milder one, to the city and society.
As much as Thoreau loved nature, he could not escape
his own ties to his fellow man or to society in general. In
1850 he wrote to his friend H. G. O. Blake, "I see less
difference between a city and a swamp than formerly."
Referring to a swamp that was too wild even for his taste,
he noted: "I prefer ever a more cultivated place, free from
miasma and crocodiles. I am so sophisticated, and I will
take my choice." While Thoreau walked in nature, he
was ever aware of its positive influence on him, but when
his walking experience was interrupted, he became
aware of a yearning for society which his walks re-
pressed: "When I have been confined to my chamber for
the greater part of several days by some employment, or
perchance by the ague, till I felt weary and house-worn, I
have been conscious of a certain softness to which I am
otherwise and commonly a stranger, in which the gates
were loosened to some emotions: and if I were to become
a confirmed invalid, I see how sympathy with mankind
and society might spring up."

Thoreau's walks never completely divorced him from
meaningful contact with his fellow men, and they were
never intended to do so. His walks returned him to the
city because he sought experiences in nature that would
enable him to function better in society upon his return.
While in nature, he separated himself from mundane
concerns, but he expected to use his nature experiences
to help himself better relate to his fellow men. His writings make clear that Thoreau was no hermit or mis-
anthrope seeking to sever himself permanently from

man: "Nature must be viewed humanly to be viewed at all; that is, her scenes must be associated with humane affections, such as are associated with one's native place, for instance. . . . A lover of Nature is preeminently a lover of man."

Thoreau lived a border existence between nature and society. Like Cooper's Natty Bumpo, Thoreau sought his moral strength from the wilderness, but he also maintained his ties with society, relating to it as best he could.

In his own writings Thoreau has much to declare about his border life between nature and society. In "Walking" he admits: "For my part, I feel that with regard to Nature I live a sort of border life, on the confines of a world into which I make occasional and transient forays only, and my patriotism and allegiance to the state into whose territories I seem to retreat are those of a moss-trooper." Affirming the role of men in his own life, he states in his *Journal:* "It is narrow to be confined to woods and fields and grand aspects of nature only. The greatest and wisest will still be related to men."

Concerning the unique quality of his experience while he walked in nature he records: "Methinks that for a great part of the time . . . I walk as one possessing the advantages of culture, fresh from the society of men, but turned loose into the woods, the only man in nature, walking and meditating to a great extent as if man and his customs and institutions were not." He also comments on the inherent tension between his attraction to nature and his ties to his fellow man: "It is with infinite yearning and aspiration that I seek solitude, more and more resolved and strong; but with a certain genial weakness that I seek society ever."

These statements, as well as Thoreau's experiences, reveal how his walking experience helped him preserve his identity by bridging the worlds of the wilderness and the city. In this respect, his sauntering paralleled his experience at Walden, where he spent a little over two years and then returned to the city as "a sojourner in civilized life again." Even while at Walden, his walking pattern followed his mutual attractions to nature and to man: "Every day or two I strolled to the village to hear some of the gossip which is incessantly going on there . . . , and which, taken in homeopathic doses, was really as refreshing in its way as the rustle of leaves and the peeping of frogs. As I walked in the woods to see the birds and squirrels, so I walked in the village to see the men and boys."

Aware that walking supplied his life with the balance he needed to relate to society, Thoreau became concerned about the issue of land usage for walkers. He worried that private land owners would so restrict their lands that walkers like himself would be unable to take rambles into nature.

Several *Journal* entries reveal Thoreau's deep sense of loss when his neighbors cut down the woods that were the haunts of so many of his walks. In January 1852 he wrote: "These woods! Why do I not feel their being cut more sorely? Does it not affect me nearly? The axe can deprive me of much. Concord is sheared of its pride. I am certainly the less attached to my native town in consequence. One, and a main, link is broken." In March of the same year, he lamented: "The woods I walked in my youth are cut off. Is it not time that I ceased to sing? My groves are invaded." Increased concern is evident in an entry three years later: "Our woods are now so reduced that the chopping of this winter has been a cutting to the quick. At least we walkers feel it as such. There is hardly a woodlot of any consequences left but the chopper's axe has been heard in it this season."

Thoreau considered this depletion of the natural environment a threat to the rights of local walkers to pursue their vocation. In "Walking" he expresses his conviction that public lands should be preserved for walkers: "At present, in this vicinity, the best part of the land is not private property; the landscape is not owned, and the walker enjoys comparative freedom. But possibly the day will come when it will be partitioned off into so-called pleasure-grounds, in which a few will take a narrow and exclusive pleasure only. . . . Let us improve our opportunities, then, before the evil days come."

Thoreau advocated the right to walk where one pleases. His independent spirit could not tolerate a restricted walking experience: "Think of a man—he may be a genius of some kind—being confined to a highway and a park for his world to range in! I should die from mere nervousness at the thought of such confinement. I should hesitate before I was born, if those terms could be made known to me beforehand. Fenced in forever by those green barriers of fields, where gentlemen are seated! Can they be said to be inhabitants of this globe? Will they be content to inhabit heaven thus partially?"

Thoreau's strongest stance on the issue of the individual right of the walker to saunter where he wishes versus the whims of the general public to use or restrict the land as they please appears in his essay "Huckleberries," which was published posthumously. In this essay he discusses his concern about the threats to the walking environment that he observed in his own time. Praising the Indian way of using the land, "common and free to all," Thoreau questioned civilization's emphasis on individual land ownership. He warns his reading public that private land ownership will eventually confine walkers to public roads and paths: "It is true, we as yet take liberties and go across lots in most directions but we naturally take fewer and fewer liberties every year, as we meet with more resistance, and we shall soon be reduced to the same straights they are in England, where going across lots is out of the question—and we must ask leave to walk in some lady's park."

In "Huckleberries" Thoreau not only laments the potential loss of the local walking environment, he also proposes that each town should do what it can to protect an adequate walking environment for its walkers: "I think that each town should have a park, or rather a primitive forest, of five hundred or a thousand acres, either in one body or several—where a stick should never be cut for fuel—nor for the navy, nor to make wagons, but stand and decay for higher uses—a common possession forever, for instruction and recreation."

Part of Thoreau's rationale for advocating the preservation of public lands for use by walkers was his belief that the value of something is determined by its use, and the highest use of something is that which caters to the individual needs of each citizen. According to his scheme of usage, land that was open to the walker, and that consequently helped meet the walker's individual needs, was more valuable than land which was excluded to the walker and used for other purposes. When describing one of his favorite walking areas, Thoreau noted: "What shall this great wild tract over which we strolled be called? Many farmers have pastures there, and wood-lots, and orchards. . . . It is a paradise for walkers in the fall. . . . It would make a princely estate in Europe, yet it is owned by farmers, who live by the labor of their hands and do not esteem it much."

Thoreau often commented on how farmers did not appreciate the true value of their land; only saunterers, by traversing the farmer's land, could sense its real transcendental value, a value greater than that yielded by the agricultural potential of the land.

Land that was plotted on a map or depicted in a real estate document held little interest for a walker like Thoreau: "How little there is on an ordinary map! How little, I mean, that concerns the walker and the lover of nature."

Thoreau viewed walking on the land as a special act tantamount to declaring ownership; when he sauntered across the fields and woods of Concord, he assumed the guise of a landowner who owned the land through the mental and spiritual act of discovery that he pursued. When sauntering, he responded to a higher law that granted ownership according to how someone used the land, and the walker used the land in the best possible way: "I affect what would commonly be called a mean and miserable way of living. I thoroughly sympathize with all savages and gypsies in so far as they merely assert the original right of man to the productions of Nature and a place in her."

Emerson, like Thoreau, sensed that the real value of the land was a matter of perspective, not legal right: "Miller owns this field, Locke that, and Manning the woodland beyond. But none of them owns the landscape. There is a property in the horizon which no man has but he whose eye can integrate all the parts, that is, the poet. This is the best part of these men's farms, yet to this their warranty-deeds give no title" ("Nature"). Thoreau was Emerson's poet, who traversed the landscape, transcendentally redeeming it as he sauntered through it: "In one light, these are old and worn-out fields that I ramble over, and men have gone to law about them long before I was born, but I trust that I ramble over them in a new fashion and redeem them."

Thoreau not only felt that the individual walker should be allowed to freely traverse the landscape and to use it as he wished, he also felt that the integrity of the individual walker should be protected against the influence of other individuals who were not walkers in the sense that Thoreau and his fellow transcendentalists were. Walking not only protected Thoreau from society collectively, it also helped him declare his individuality against the potential encroachments of other individuals.

Solitude was a key part of Thoreau's walking experience because during his walks he attempted to empty himself of all that was not truly himself. Solitude was the condition which most fed his soul: "I thrive best on solitude. If I had a companion only one day a week, unless it were one or two I could name, I find that the value of the week to me has been seriously affected." In a letter to his friend, Daniel Ricketson, Thoreau confessed: "As some heads cannot carry much wine, so it would seem that I cannot bear so much society as you can. I have an immense appetite for solitude, like an infant for sleep, and if I don't get enough of it this year I shall cry all the next."

Thoreau considered his walking time sacred, and he was reluctant to share it with anyone else. His walks not only carried him away from the city, they also carried him away from other individuals who wished to share them with him. Charles Woodbury recollects how Thoreau, when asked by others if they could walk with him, would reply: "'Ah, walking—that is my holy time.'" The strength of Thoreau's commitment to preserve his integrity during his walking experience against the encroachments of others is convincingly clear in this *Journal* entry: "I am invited to take some party of ladies or gentlemen on an excursion,—to walk or sail, or the like,—but by all kinds of evasions I omit it, and am thought to be rude and unaccommodating therefore. They do not consider that the woodpath and the boat are my studio, while I maintain a sacred solitude and cannot admit promiscuous company. . . . They do not think of taking a child away from its school to go a-huckleberrying with them. Why should not I, then, have my school and school hours to be respected? Ask me for a certain number of dollars if you will, but do not ask me for my afternoons."

Thoreau preferred the freedom that solitary rambling afforded: "I do not know if I am singular when I say that I believe there is no man with whom I can associate who will not, comparatively speaking, spoil my afternoon. That society or encounter may at last yield a fruit which I am not aware of, but I cannot help suspecting that I should have spent those hours more profitably alone."

Emerson depicted the typical transcendentalist as one who "goes to walk alone," but he does so, not "from any whim" but "from temperament and from principle." Thoreau expressed a similar sentiment in a letter he wrote to his friend Blake: "It is not that we love to be alone, but that we love to soar, and when we do soar, the company grows thinner & thinner till there is none at all."

Thoreau persisted in putting space between himself and others in order to protect his integrity: "Often, I would rather undertake to shoulder a barrel of pork and carry it a mile than take into my company a man. It would not be so heavy a weight upon my mind. I could put it down and only feel my back ache for it."

Thoreau was not completely opposed to a walking companion, but he frequently expressed his frustration with trying to find a walking companion who would truly be a kindred spirit. He recognized that true walking involves more than simply physically traveling the same course. Unless the walkers travel the same path in their minds, companionship is detrimental to the walking experience: "Now at least the moon is full, and I walk alone, which is best by night, if not by day always. Your companion must sympathize with the present mood. The conversation must be located where the walkers are, and vary exactly with the scene and events and the contour of the ground. Farewell to those who will talk of nature unnaturally, whose presence is an interruption." Thoreau disdained the company of those whose manners and spirit made them inappropriate walking companions: "With most the walk degenerates into a mere vigorous use of your legs, ludicrously purposeless, while you are discussing some mighty argument, each one having his say, spoiling each other's day, worrying one another with conversation, hustling one another with our conversation. I know of no use in the walking part in this case."

Because Thoreau found it so difficult to find a kindred spirit to share his walks with, it should not be surprising that he used walking as a metaphor to express his frustrated desires for companionship in his own life: "What if we feel a yearning to which no breast answers? I walk alone. . . . I knock on the earth for my friend. I expect to meet him at every turn; but no friend appears, and perhaps none is dreaming of me. . . . I would fain walk on the deep waters, but my companions will only walk on shallows and puddles."

When walking, Thoreau found in nature the kindred spirit that he often failed to discover in his fellow man. Walking in the outdoors soothed him and touched his inner being in a way that the most genuine friendship might. "By my intimacy with nature I find myself withdrawn from man. My interest in the sun and the moon, in the morning and the evening, compels me to solitude. . . ."

So important were Thoreau's ties to nature that he jealously guarded his relationship with nature against the potential encroachments of human society: "I am sure that if I call for a companion in my walk I have relinquished in my design some closeness of communion with Nature. The walk will surely be more commonplace. The inclination for society indicates a distance from Nature. I do not design so wild and mysterious a walk." The tensions between human companionship and intercourse with nature surface in a January 1857 reflection: "I was describing the other day my success in solitary and distant woodland walking outside the town. I do not go there to get my dinner, but to get that sustenance which dinners only preserve me to enjoy, without which dinners are a vain repetition. But how little men can help me in this! only by having a kindred experience. . . . I never chanced to meet with any man so cheering and elevating, so infinitely suggestive, as the stillness and solitude of the Well Meadow Field."

Nature was not the only form of companionship that Thoreau experienced during his rambles. He also found his imagination and thoughts to be fit companions. In *Walden* Thoreau describes how he would project himself mentally outside of himself to provide a second self for companionship during a walk: "I only know myself as a human entity; the scene, so to speak, of thoughts and affections; and am sensible of a certain doubleness by which I can stand as remote from myself as from another. However intense my experience, I am conscious of the presence and criticism of a part of me, which, as it were, is not a part of me, but spectator, sharing no experience, but taking note of it, and that is no more I than it is you." In his *Journal* Thoreau observes: "My thoughts are my company. They have a certain individuality and separate existence, aye, personality."

Thoreau could carry this notion of the separate life of thoughts to an extreme, equating the echo of his voice with the thoughts of another person. Such was the case during one of his winter walks when, using his voice to echo messages through the woods, he concluded: "It was a profounder Socratic method of suggesting thoughts unutterable to me the speaker. There was one I heartily loved to talk with. Under such favorable auspices I could converse with myself, could reflect; the hour, the atmosphere, and the conformation of the ground permitted it."

Because they refreshed him and strengthened his sense of identity, Thoreau's jaunts nourished his social life, equipping him to deal better with the world of men. He was not as lost in the world of human society as his *Journal* entries would have us believe. Bronson Alcott's testimony refutes the view that Thoreau shunned close ties to others: "Friendly he is, and holds his friends by bearings as strict in their tenderness and consideration as are the laws of his thinking,—as prompt and kindly equitable,—neighborly always, and as apt for occasions as he is strenuous against meddling with others in things not his" ("The Forester"). Samuel Higginson, a younger contemporary of Thoreau's, shares a similar portrait: "It was with joy that we hailed our first approach to this man, and gradually came to know more in regard to his private life. As our acquaintance grew, we found him to be one of the rarest companions, beneath whose rugged exterior there lay a lively appreciation of all that is vivifying in nature, and a natural yearning toward his fellowmen, together with a kindly sympathy, which was but the basis of his simple philosophy."

Thoreau's walking experience reveals not only the tensions inherent in his own life between the pull of nature and the pull of society, it also demonstrates his inability to fully resolve the conflicts he experienced between his desire for solitude and his yearning for meaningful human companionship. This conflict provides the focus for an April 1852 *Journal* entry: "I have got to that pass with my friend that our words do not pass with each other for what they are worth. We speak in vain; there is none to hear. He finds fault with me that I walk alone, when I pine for want of a companion; that I commit my thoughts to a diary even on my walks; instead of seeking to share them generously with a friend; curses my practice even. Awful as it is to contemplate, I pray that, if I am the cold intellectual skeptic whom he rebukes, his curse may take effect, and wither and dry up those sources of my life, and my journal no longer yield me pleasure nor life."

In *Walden* Thoreau assessed his own sociability more positively than many others have since his day: "I think that I love society as much as most, and am ready enough to fasten myself like a bloodsucker for the time to any full-blooded man that comes in my way. I am naturally no hermit, but might possibly sit out the sturdiest frequenter of the bar-room, if my business called me thither."

Thoreau's aversion to having a walking companion was not due to any desire on his part to shun company; rather, he had a difficult time finding a walking partner who would meet the high standard that he set for himself and any who would travel with him. To find someone to saunter with who would not interfere with his walk nor oppress his spirit was a challenging task. John Burroughs, a fellow walker and contemporary of Thoreau, explains the difficulties inherent in selecting a good walking partner: "Every lover of Nature understands Thoreau's aversion to a companion on a walk, except he be a true lover also. It is a rare qualification to be a good walker. We do not go to the woods for society, or to talk politics; and he that would go with me, must leave me to myself, and leave the town behind him. . . . You do not want to be diverted or hindered, but open."

In addition to the qualms about potential walkers that Burroughs mentions, Thoreau made clear that anyone wishing to walk with him would have to be willing to take a long walk. He had no tolerance for would-be saunterers who were interested only in brief, short rambles: "I do not know how to entertain one who can't take long walks. . . . I give up my forenoon to them and get along pretty well, the very elasticity of the air and promise of the day abetting me, but they are as heavy as dumplings by mid-afternoon. If they can't walk, why won't they take an honest nap and let me go in the afternoon?"

One Concordian who Thoreau did allow to saunter with him testified to Thoreau's lack of tolerance for those who could not handle the rigors of the walking experience: "He was ready to open that side of himself to any one who w[oul]d pay the price. But that meant, to go w[ith] him in his walk; to walk long & far; to h[a]v[e] wet feet & go so for hours; to pull a boat all day & to come home late at night after many miles. If you w[oul]d do that w[ith] him, he w[oul]d take you w[ith] him. If you flinched at anyth[in]g, he had no more use for you" (Burgess.)

Although Thoreau sought walking companions who proved as hardy as himself, his primary concern was that a walking partner be one in mind and spirit with himself. In *A Week* he notes that "if two travellers would go their way harmoniously together, the one must take as true and just a view of things as the other, else their path will not be strewn with roses." Thoreau focused one of his poems on his deeply felt desire to walk with someone of a kindred spirit:

> I walk in nature still alone
>   And know no one
> Discern no lineament nor feature
>   Of any creature.
>
> Though all the firmament
>   Is o'er me bent,
> Yet still I miss the grace
>   Of an intelligent and kindred face.
>
> I still must seek the friend
> Who does with nature blend,
> Who is the person in her mask,
> He is the man I ask.
>
> Who is the expression of her meaning,
> Who is the uprightness of her leaning,
> Who is the grown child of her weaning
>
> . . . .

> We twain would walk together
> Through every weather,
> And see this aged nature,
> Go with a bending stature.

Although Thoreau sought a walking companion as a kindred spirit, he did not look for someone who could not think for himself. The purpose of the walk, after all, was to protect and nurture the private self of each walker. In one *Journal* observation, Thoreau expressed his delight in "loafers, fishers, and hunters" who he encountered during his walks. What marked them from the others was that they did "not go out of themselves to meet" Thoreau. Others, who adjusted or altered themselves in an effort to please Thoreau, offended him: "I am bothered to walk with those who wish to keep step with me. It is not necessary to keep step with your companion, as some endeavor to do."

Thoreau also insisted that walking partners be able to forsake society during the walking experience. A good walker should be able to reap the full benefits of a walk by emptying himself of all thoughts and associations with the city that he has left behind: "How rarely I meet with a man who can be free, even in thought! We live according to rule. Some men are bedridden; all, world-ridden. I take my neighbor, an intellectual man, out into the woods and invite him to take a new and absolute view of things, to empty clean out of his thoughts all institutions of men and start again; but he can't do it, he sticks to his traditions and his crotchets. He thinks that governments, colleges, newspapers, etc., are from everlasting to everlasting."

Since it is easier for common men to forsake society than it is for affluent or important men to do so, Thoreau preferred taking his most serious walks with common men: "I have several friends and acquaintances who are very good companions in the house or for an afternoon walk, but whom I cannot make up my mind to make a longer excursion with; for I discover, all at once, that they are too gentlemanly in manners, dress, and all their habits. . . . You should travel as a common man."

Thoreau also preferred walking companions who were good listeners: "He was a capital guide in the wood. . . . I do not think he was vain. But he liked to do his thinking out loud, and expected that you should be an auditor rather than a companion" (Hoar). *Journal* entries reveal that a compatible walking partner would also be patient—"I regretted that I had an impatient companion"—and morally upright—"I am made somewhat sad this afternoon by the coarseness and vulgarity of my companion."

In spite of Thoreau's high standard for a walking companion and his need for solitude, he frequently walked with others. Ellery Channing, Thoreau's most consistent walking companion, claimed that Thoreau had frequent offers by others to accompany him on walks, and that he often accepted them. Walter Harding, more cautious in his estimate of how often Thoreau shared his walking experience with others, notes that Thoreau did allow a few of his close friends to walk with him because he trusted them not to interfere with the private nature of his walking experience.

Relatives and close friends comprised one group of people with whom Thoreau frequently sauntered. When Thoreau was younger, his brother, John, served as his faithful companion during his ramblings. In an early essay, "Musings," Thoreau reminisced: "In the freshness of the dawn my brother and I were ready to enjoy a stroll to a certain cliff, distant a mile or more, where we were wont to climb to the highest peak" (*Early Essays*). Thoreau's sister, Helen, also provided him with a welcome walking partner.

Though not a relative, Ellen Sewall, Thoreau's only real romantic interest, took a number of walks with him. Other nonrelatives also enjoyed a consistent and meaningful relationship with Thoreau during his walks. Foremost among these individuals was William Ellery Channing. Thoreau's *Journal* and correspondence, as illustrated in the following excerpts, contain numerous references to walks taken with Channing: "Met Channing and walked with him to what we will call Grackle Swamp"; "More recently I have taken an interesting walk with Channing about Cape Ann"; and "Called to C[hanning] from the outside of his house the other afternoon in the rain. At length he put his head out the attic window, and I inquired if he didn't want to take a walk."

Thoreau's close friend, Ralph Waldo Emerson, also took frequent walks with Thoreau. Emerson counted these excursions a special privilege. Bronson Alcott, like Emerson, was a close friend and transcendentalist who accompanied Thoreau on several walks, although Alcott's penchant for philosophical discussion and reflection at times hindered Thoreau's walking experience. Thoreau enjoyed some memorable walks with Alcott, including the exhilarating one described in the following *Journal* entry, which depicts a Platonic meeting of the minds, a bonding of two spirits during the walking experience: "It has occurred to me, while I am thinking with pleasure of our day's intercourse, 'Why should I not think aloud to you?' Having each some shingles of thought well dried, we walk and whittle them, trying our knives, and admiring the clear yellowish grain of the pumpkin pine. We wade so gently and reverently, or we pull together so smoothly, that the fishes of thought are not scared from the stream, but come and go grandly, like yonder clouds that float peacefully through the western sky. When we walk it seems as if the heavens . . . and the earth had met together, and righteousness and peace kissed each other."

Although his family and close friends frequently accompanied him on his rambles, Thoreau also shared his walking experience with less familiar figures. In his recollection of Thoreau, Moncure Conway observes, "A day or two later, however, I enjoyed my first walk with Thoreau which was succeeded by many others." In a letter to Thoreau, Daniel Ricketson recalled the rambles they had shared together: "I look back with pleasure upon my late visit to Concord. The particular bright spots are my walks with you to Farmer Hosmer's and to Walden Pond, as well as our visit to friend Alcott" (*Correspondence*). In a letter to Ricketson, Thoreau mentioned, "A young English author, Thomas Cholmondeley, is just now waiting for me to take a walk with him—therefore excuse this very barren note" (*Correspondence*). Walking was often on Thoreau's mind when he corresponded with his acquaintances, as the following lines from a letter to Jones Very suggest: "I shall improve or take an opportunity to spend a day—or part of a day with you ere long, and I trust that you will be attracted to Concord again, and will find me a better walker than I chanced to be when you were here before." He then adds, "I have often thought of taking a walk with you in your vicinity" (*Correspondence*).

Several *Journal* entries indicate that Thoreau walked with a wide variety of individuals, although he walked regularly with only a few. Sample entries are: "Rice, who walks with me, thinks that the fine early sedge grass would be a capital thing to stuff cushions and beds with"; and "5 A.M.—Walk with Blake, Brown, and Rogers to Quinsigamond Pond, carrying our breakfast."

Although he preferred walking alone, it seems clear that Thoreau often walked with others, sharing walking experiences with them while carefully protecting his own private experience from any threatening intrusions. His walks helped him assert his own individuality against the threatening encroachments of society, collectively, and certain people, individually. But they did not deprive him of the human fellowship which he required as much as he did solitude and a contact with nature.

Walking provided Thoreau with complete social satisfaction as he enjoyed intercourse with nature, his own thoughts, and carefully selected walking companions. Thus, the self, the most important thing to Thoreau, found its fulfillment in the rambles that he took nearly every day of his adult life.

5

THE QUEST FOR VOCATION

Walking served a higher purpose for Thoreau than merely equipping him to assert his self against the influences and encroachments of society. Sauntering also provided him with a way to satisfy his need for a vocation and for artistic expression. Sauntering appealed to Thoreau's practical and idealistic sides, making possible the kind of personal growth and creative expression that his essential self required. Walking satisfied Thoreau's quest for a vocation in several ways. His sauntering life directly affected his views on the jobs he held like surveying and lecturing, it influenced his adherence to a work ethic that contrasted sharply with that of his contemporaries, and it functioned as an integral part of his writing experience, helping him convert experience into reflection and written observation. Walking helped satisfy Thoreau's strong desire to have a vocation that would cater to his personal needs.

One of the real quandaries that Thoreau faced throughout his adult life was the issue of vocation. Because self-reliance was so important to him, and because he advocated a nonmaterialistic apporach to life, most vocations or jobs seemed unpromising or unfulfilling to Thoreau. Thoreau detested working for others, or for money. He worked when he had to, in order to supply his most basic wants: he taught school, made pencils in his parents' pencil factory, surveyed, lectured, and wrote; but none of these activities fulfilled him in the way that walking did.

Sauntering in nature provided Thoreau with a form of self-employment that superseded the material benefits he gained from his more regular jobs. Rather than hold a regular job, Thoreau devoted the majority of his time to sauntering; sauntering became, in a sense, his vocation, or more accurately, his avocation. That he considered walking his "vocation" seems clear in the following *Journal* observation: "No doubt my dusty and tawny cowhides surprise the street walkers who wear patent-leather or Congress shoes, but they do not consider how absurd such shoes would be in my vocation, to thread the woods and swamps in."

Thoreau took walking as seriously as most of his contemporaries took their own vocations, but he did not consider his sauntering as equivalent to everyday work. For Thoreau, walking was something higher and more noble than the mere sustaining of life by a particular wage-earning activity. He shares his feelings about this in *A Week* when he observes: "But I never thought of travelling simply as a means of getting a livelihood. . . . True and serious travelling is no pastime, but it is as serious as the grave, or any other part of the human journey, and it requires a long probation to be broken into it."

Thoreau's biographers have commented on the work-like nature of Thoreau's walking experience. Notes Channing: "He did not walk with any view to health, or exercise, or amusement. . . . *No, the walk, with him, was for work; it had a serious purpose.*" Canby observes, "These daily excursions were business for him, and though he heartily enjoyed them, he was at work every instant."

For Thoreau, the most important consideration in the choice of a vocation was how a particular vocation would affect one's self. Any activity that fulfilled the self he esteemed; any activity that did not directly touch the life of the self he disdained. He discusses his philosophy in a March 1853 *Journal* entry: "It is essential that a man confine himself to pursuits—a scholar, for instance, to studies—which lie next to and conduce his life, which do not go against the grain, either of his will or his imagination." Later, in the same year, Thoreau queried: "What other liberty is there worth having, if we have not freedom and peace in our minds,—if our inmost and most private man is but a sour and turbid pool?" In Wordsworthian fashion, he responded to his own question by lamenting: "Ah! the world is too much with us, and our whole soul is stained by what it works in, like the dyer's hand. A man had better starve at once than lose his innocence in the process of getting his bread."

Thoreau valued his personal freedom. Walking offered him the freedom he needed to pursue the concerns of the self, and it avoided the pitfalls of other vocations that threatened one's personal freedom. In *Walden* he observed, "As I preferred some things to others, and especially valued my freedom, as I could fare hard and yet succeed well, I did not wish to spend my time in earning rich carpets or other fine furniture, or delicate cookery, or a house in the Grecian or the Gothic style just yet."

Once, when walking down a country road, Thoreau met a fellow saunterer, an old man, who epitomized in his demeanor the type of vocational experience that Thoreau most desired. This aging citizen of Concord appeared to be simply out walking in nature, discovering what he could as he rambled about. Thoreau's *Journal* reveals the pleasure he derived from considering this man's approach to "vocation": "I was glad of an occasion to suspect that this afternoon he had not been at 'work' but living somewhat after my own fashion. . . . [He] had been out to see what nature had for him, and now was hastening home to a burrow he knew, where he could warm his old feet."

Thoreau wished to be like this elderly saunterer, one who could follow his good genius, walking about the countryside as he wished, and ignoring societal expectations about regular work hours and wage-earning ability.

The closest Thoreau came to being a respectable laborer, from his contemporaries' point of view, was when he undertook the job of surveyor. Surveying, which involved a great deal of walking, and which usually placed him in nature, offered him a compromise vocation. Although it did not entirely satisfy him, surveying allowed him to earn enough money to maintain his simple existence and to range outside the stifling environment of the city.

In spite of Thoreau's resentment that material necessities forced him to work for others and that surveying limited his personal freedom to saunter for his own purposes, this occupation did offer him important advantages over other potential forms of employment. Surveying kept Thoreau outdoors and provided him with opportunities to appreciate flora and fauna while being paid to do so. He surveyed several weeks each year and had the rest of the year to pursue his own goals. Surveying offered Thoreau a way to earn money and sustain himself while freeing many of his days for sauntering and other desirable pursuits.

Although surveying restricted the way that he found things in nature, the discoveries Thoreau did make while surveying helped compensate for the fact that he was working for someone else. In a December 1857 *Journal* entry, Thoreau reflects on one discovery he made while surveying: "Even this is a cheering and compensating discovery in my otherwise barren work. I get thus a few positive values, answering to the bread and cheese which make my dinner. I owe thus to my weeks at surveying a few such slight but positive discoveries." Surveying offered certain advantages, however slight Thoreau might have considered them.

Regardless of what occupation Thoreau would have

attempted, he would have been dissatisfied because any vocation, even surveying, sacrificed his personal freedom and tied him to the material world that he sought to retreat from during his saunters. Surveying was a necessary evil that made possible some time, but never enough time, for sauntering.

The world of work cast a pall over Thoreau like the black veil which hung over the minister's face in Hawthorne's story, "The Minister's Black Veil." Thoreau wrote in his *Journal:* "I thought to walk this forenoon instead of this afternoon, for I have not been in the fields and woods much of late except when surveying, but the least affair of that kind is as if you had [a] black veil drawn over your face which shut out nature, as that eccentric and melancholy minister whom I have heard of. It may be the fairest day in all the year and you shall not know it. One little chore to do, one little commission to fulfill, one message to carry, would spoil heaven itself. Talk about a lover being engaged! He is the only man in all the world who is free. And all you get is your dollars."

Thoreau's *Journal* reveals how his walks functioned as welcome retreats from society, while the practical world of work presented unwelcome withdrawals from the world of nature that he sought during his walks: "After spending four or five days surveying and drawing a plan incessantly, I especially feel the necessity of putting myself in communication with nature again, to recover my tone, to withdraw out of the wearying and unprofitable world of affairs."

In an earlier *Journal* entry Thoreau also confesses his desire to escape the shallow, materialistic work world represented by surveying and to saunter freely into the world of nature: "I have been surveying for twenty or thirty days, living coarsely . . . —indeed, leading a quite trivial life; and to-night, for the first time, had made a fire in my chamber and endeavored to return to myself.

I wished to ally myself to the powers that rule the universe. I wished to dive into some deep stream of thoughtful and devoted life, which meandered through retired and fertile meadows far from towns. . . . I wished for leisure and quiet to let my life flow in its proper channels, with its proper currents; when I might not waste the days, might establish daily prayer and thanksgiving in my family; might do my own work and not the work of Concord and Carlisle, which would yield me better than money."

Thoreau tried lecturing as a way to combine his interests with a way to support himself, but this also proved disappointing. He wanted to lecture, but he found far more opportunities to survey: "I have offered myself much more earnestly as a lecturer than a surveyor. Yet I do not get any employment as a lecturer; was not invited to lecture once last winter, and only once (without pay) this winter. But I can get surveying enough." In time, Thoreau had the opportunity to give a number of lectures, talks that often dealt with subjects dear to his heart. His essay "Walking" was born from two lectures that he presented—one dealing with the idea of sauntering and one touching on the qualities of the wild that so attracted him. But even lecturing on these important themes did little to satisfy him since the lecturing experience was engaged in for monetary gain. In a letter to his friend, Daniel Ricketson, Thoreau confessed his frustration at trying to earn a living while wanting to live the kind of life that would deny material motivation for one's actions. He had difficulty resolving the division in his life between the world of work and the world of sauntering in nature: "I should like right well to see your ponds, but that is hardly to be thought of at present. I fear that it is impossible *for me* to combine such things with the business of lecturing. You cannot serve God and Mammon."

Walking in nature was the only "work" that Thoreau

consistently committed himself to that fulfilled and rewarded him. For this work he earned a higher wage than the dollars for which his contemporaries labored.

Sauntering in nature was Thoreau's way of attempting to avoid the curse of work that God afflicted on Adam in the Garden of Eden. Because of his sin, Adam was banished from the Garden and informed that he and all future men would have to subsist by the sweat of their brows (Genesis 3:17–19). Thoreau's walks returned him to the innocent world of the garden, which knew only the honest sweat drawn from a life in nature, not the corrupted sweat of the world of work. In an early essay, "Commercial Spirit," Thoreau expressed his desire to escape the curse of work by sauntering daily in nature, enjoying the sabbath experience of a life without toil and care: "The order of things should be somewhat reversed,—the seventh should be man's day of toil, wherein to earn his living by the sweat of his brow, and the other six his sabbath of the affections and the soul, in which to range this wide-spread garden, and drink in the soft influences and sublime revelations of Nature" (*Early Essays*).

For Thoreau, a man's life was not to be measured by his means to get a living, but rather by the life he lived. He considered his vocation not those jobs he held for pay, but those activities like sauntering which made his life a pastime and a pleasure. This is quite clear in *Walden* when Thoreau, after leaving the cabin of an impoverished Irishman, found himself first questioning, and then, reaffirming his commitment to a life of freely sauntering in nature: "As I was leaving the Irishman's roof after the rain, bending my steps again to the pond, my haste to catch pickerel, wading in retired meadows, in sloughs and bogholes, in forlorn and savage places, appeared for an instant trivial to me who had been sent to school and college; but as I ran down the hill toward the reddening west, with the rainbow over my shoulder, and some faint tinkling sounds borne to my ear through the cleansed air, from I know not what quarter, my Good Genius seemed to say,—Go fish and hunt far and wide day by day,— farther and wider,—and rest thee by many brooks and hearth-sides without misgiving. Remember thy Creator in the days of thy youth. Rise free from care before the dawn, and seek adventures. Let the noon find thee by other lakes, and the night overtake thee every where at home. There are no larger fields than these, no worthier games than may here be played. Grow wild according to thy nature, like these sedges and brakes, which will never become English hay. . . . Let not to get a living be thy trade, but thy sport. Enjoy the land, but own it not. Through want of enterprise and faith men are where they are, buying and selling, and spending their lives like serfs."

Thoreau enjoyed hard work. But he resented working hard for someone else; he detested having to earn money when he felt that life had so many better things to offer him.

Concentrating on work, even outdoor work, rather than giving oneself to the glories of a day, seemed unforgivable to Thoreau. He observed in his *Journal:* "The mass of mankind, who live in houses or shops, or are *bent* upon their labor out of doors, know nothing of the beautiful days which are passing about them. Is not such a day worthy of a hymn?" Thoreau devoted his life to beautiful days, not to labor: "I have given myself up to nature; I have lived so many springs and summers and autumns and winters as if I had nothing else to do but *live* them, and imbibe whatever nutriment they had for me."

The contrast between Thoreau's sauntering life in nature and the everyday work world that he was sometimes forced to participate in provides the focus of a December 1854 *Journal* reflection: "Winter has come unnoticed by me, I have been so busy writing. This is the life most lead in respect to Nature. How different from my habitual one! It is hasty, coarse, and trivial, as if you were a spindle in a factory. The other is leisurely, fine, and glorious, like a flower. In the first case you are merely getting your living; in the second you are living as you go along."

Few men of Thoreau's own day appreciated his perspective. The materialistic bent of Concord society made Thoreau's quest for a nonmaterialistic vocation a difficult and unpopular one. Many artists of Thoreau's time experienced rejection by society and resorted to walking or traveling to make their art possible. In fact, the less accepted the artist, the more likely that he would be a walker. This was certainly the case with Thoreau, whose rejection by society led him to sauntering away from it.

Thoreau defended a naturalist vocation against the prevailing sentiment of his time that a life devoted to studying nature was wasteful. He grew up in a New England society that had always questioned the value of walking in nature. But Thoreau questioned the Puritan ethic upon which New England society was founded. Why would one shun a sauntering life in order to demean himself by working in the accepted way to earn a living? This was the question he posed in his essay, "Huckleberries," applying it to those English naturalists who apologized for their work in nature: "I have observed that many English naturalists have a pitiful habit of speaking of their proper pursuit as a sort of trifling or waste of time—a mere interruption to more important employments and 'severer studies'—for which they must ask pardon of the reader. As if they would have you believe that all the rest of their lives was consecrated to some truly great and serious enterprise. . . . Comparatively speaking—what they call their graver pursuits and severer studies was the real trifling and misspense of life—and were they such fools as not to know it?"

Thoreau fiercely defended his sauntering life against

the charges of others that he was a loafer and unproductive member of society. In "Life Without Principle" he adamantly expresses his sense of the emptiness and futility of a life of commercial labor when contrasted with the fulfillment and rewards of the sauntering life: "Perhaps I am more than usually jealous with respect to my freedom. I feel that my connection with and obligation to society are still very slight and transient. . . . If I should sell both my forenoons and afternoons to society, as most appear to do, I am sure, that, for me, there would be nothing left worth living for. I trust that I shall never thus sell my birthright for a mess of pottage. I wish to suggest that a man may be very industrious, and yet not spend his time well. There is no more fatal blunderer than he who consumes the greater part of his life getting his living. All great enterprises are self-supporting" (*Reform Papers*).

Walking was the only activity that allowed Thoreau to follow his good genius, to be about his own business rather than someone else's business. This, too, was very important to him: "If you would really take a position outside the street and daily life of men, you must have deliberately planned your course, you must have business which is not your neighbors' business, which they cannot understand. . . . You will spend this afternoon in setting up your neighbor's stove, and be paid for it; I will spend it in gathering the few berries of the *Vaccinium Oxycoccus* which Nature produces here, before it is too late, and *be paid for it also* after another fashion. I have always reaped unexpected and incalculable advantages from carrying out at last, however tardily, any little enterprise which my genius suggested to me long ago as a thing to be done,—some step to be taken, however slight, out of the usual course."

Thoreau's neighbors generally misunderstood his walks, as they did the philosophical and transcendental ideas that formed the foundation of his walking experience. So private and so nonconformist in nature were Thoreau's rambles, that neighbors or strangers alike had trouble understanding why he spent so much time walking in nature: "I see that my neighbors look with compassion on me, that they think it is a mean and unfortunate destiny which makes me to walk these fields and woods so much and sail on this river alone. But so long as I find here the only real elysium, I cannot hesitate in my choice." Even Thoreau's Aunt Maria protested, "'I wish [he] could find something better to do than walking off every now and then'" (Harding, *Days*). Typical of how his contemporaries viewed his saunters is this statement made by Frank Pierce: "He was a queer kind of a duck. Always used to wear a gray shirt and tramp through the woods every day" (Whitcomb, "The Thoreau 'Country'"). When Pierce tried to guess why Thoreau walked so much, he concluded that Thoreau did it for his health (Thomas), a conclusion that missed the mark by a considerable distance. Most people who encountered Thoreau on his walks failed to understand the purpose of his rambles. One Staten Island resident concluded that Thoreau was walking about the island for the sake of land speculation. He could not be convinced that Thoreau was doing so much walking with no commercial purpose in mind. In fact, he tried to hire Thoreau to help him sell his farm.

Considering Thoreau a land speculator was a compliment compared to what many contemporaries assumed about the motives for Thoreau's walks. Some were quick to label him as a peddler. Others drew more radical conclusions. When Thoreau and Channing sauntered on Cape Cod in June 1850, a local policeman and some of the local residents suspected them of being bank robbers because a bank was robbed a few days after their passing through the area. In *Cape Cod* Thoreau responded to this in good humor: "But the only bank that we pried into was the great Cape Cod sand-bank, and we robbed it only of an old French crown piece, some shells and pebbles, and the materials of this story." Thoreau certainly needed a sense of humor to deal with the conclusions others drew about his walks. When one farmer spotted Thoreau standing for an extended period of time in a pool of water, he decided that Thoreau was the farmer's own father who had been "drinking some of Pat Haggerty's rum, and had lost his way home." When the farmer went to help his drunk father out, he discovered to his chagrin that his father was elsewhere and Thoreau was simply out on one of his walks examining nature in typical but misunderstood fashion.

Because his walking experience was so misunderstood, Thoreau's friends, and even later critics, tended to judge his life a failure. Emerson concluded that Thoreau "had no ambition," and that his only real achievement was to be "the captain of a huckleberry party" ("Thoreau"). Some felt, like Robert Louis Stevenson, that Thoreau approached life with a "womanish solicitude," that his seeming unmanliness arose from his fear of contact with human society. Thus, "in one word, Thoreau was a skulker" ("Thoreau"). James Russell Lowell shared a similar view, accusing Thoreau of being too provincial and too unnatural in his seeming rejection of civilization in favor of walking in the woods: "We do not believe that the way to a true cosmopolitanism carries one into the woods or the society of musquashes. Perhaps the narrowest provincialism is that of Self" ("Thoreau").

Certainly Lowell was right to comment on Thoreau's obsession with the self, for self culture was the focus of Thoreau's saunterings. Thoreau cared very little what his contemporaries thought about him, but he cared very much about his own needs and aspirations. His walks, so misunderstood by others, were designed to meet the needs of the self, including the need for self-expression. Thoreau was a true artist, with an artistic temperament, and he felt a genuine need to express himself in artistic form. Writing, much more than lecturing or conversing, provided him with an effective form of self-expression, and he used his walking experience to give shape and meaning to his writings.

Thoreau combined walking and writing into a hybrid vocation which uniquely matched his own needs. His need to walk in nature was paralleled by his need to write about his walks in nature. As an artist, he sought to convert his sauntering experiences into written accounts which tapped the real significance of his saunters.

Writing, current composition theorists inform us, is an act of discovery. When we write, we discover our true feelings and thoughts about the writing subject. This was certainly the case with Thoreau, who knew that the discovery process of his walks was incomplete until he had a chance to write about his walks. Thoreau's advice to his friend H. G. O. Blake concerning how to write about a mountain climb that Blake had undertaken reveals his attitude about the important role that writing plays in capping the walking experience: "Let me suggest a theme for you: to state to yourself precisely and completely what that walk over the mountains amounted to for you,—returning to this essay again and again, until you are satisfied that all that was important in your experience is in it."

The very act of walking, as Thoreau was well aware, improves one's ability to write well; the physical movement that walking entails stimulates not only the blood's circulation, but also one's thoughts and feelings. Thoreau found it necessary to walk, to move, in order to write: "How vain it is to sit down to write when you have not stood up to live! Methinks that the moment my legs begin to move, my thoughts begin to flow, as if I had given vent to the stream at the lower end and consequently new fountains flowed into it at the upper. . . . Only while we are in action is the circulation perfect. The writing which consists with habitual sitting is mechanical, wooden, dull to read."

Thoreau could not produce the kind of prose he aimed at unless his legs had been in motion, and his thoughts free and flowing. Ralph Waldo Emerson, Thoreau's good friend and mentor, stated that Thoreau depended in his writing experience on "every stride his legs made. The length of his walk uniformly made the length of his writing. If shut up in the house, he did not write at all" ("Thoreau"). As Stevenson observes, "Exercise and composition were . . . intimately connected" for Thoreau.

Most writers have been aware, as Thoreau was, of the integral relationship between physical activity and good writing. Like Thoreau, numerous authors have walked in order to lubricate their thinking processes and free those thoughts trapped in their subconscious minds which, when expressed, create the most telling effect or make the most profound impression on the reader. Thoreau's walking/writing experience was soundly grounded in a cooperative adventure of mind and body working harmoniously together to produce the most meaningful experience. He observes: "We cannot write well or truly but what we write with gusto. The body, the senses, must conspire with the mind. Expression is the act of the whole man, that our speech may be vascular. The intellect is powerless to express thought without the aid of the heart and liver and of every member."

With this kind of cooperative activity between mind and body, Thoreau was able to enter a special psychological state during his saunterings, which resulted in the mental discoveries that fill the pages of his writing. His sauntering induced his subconscious mind to release his thoughts, the result of free-play between his body, his mind, and the environment. According to Zwinger, the mental state that Thoreau would often enter we know today as the Alpha state—a state where the saunterer experiences "a heightened awareness and sensitivity, an increased intellectual ability and alertness, yet with a feeling of relaxation and ease, an effortless flowing of creativity, and a sense of remoteness from the everyday world." When Thoreau sauntered, "he entered his own Alpha state. In other words, when Thoreau hit his stride as a wanderer, he hit his stride as a writer. He must have learned early on, of the psychological beneficence of wandering, that when his eye was busy, his mind was free to play with new connections and perceptions."

Thoreau's *Journal* record of one particular walk describes what for him was a typical Alpha state experience: "You must walk so gently as to hear the finest sounds, the faculties being in repose. Your mind must not perspire. True, out of doors my thought is commonly drowned, as it were, and shrunken, pressed down by stupendous piles of light ethereal influences, for the pressure of the atmosphere is still fifteen pounds to a square inch. I can do little more than preserve the equilibrium and resist the pressure of the atmosphere. I can only nod like the rye-heads in the breeze. I expand more surely in my chamber, as far as expression goes, as if that pressure were taken off; but here outdoors is the place to store up influences." As this entry reveals, Thoreau's subconscious mind preserved "influences" during the walk that later reflection would convert into conscious, written observations.

Thoreau, however, did not wait until he returned home from a walk to begin his writing. He took profuse notes of his experiences during his walks. These notes aided his memory when he later attempted to recall his sauntering experiences.

Channing, Thoreau's most faithful walking companion, provides the most detailed description of this part of Thoreau's writing process: "Abroad, he used the pencil, writing but a few moments at a time, during the walk; but into the note-book must go all measurements with the foot-rule which he always carried, or the surveyor's tape that he often had with him. Also all observations with his spyglass . . . , all conditions of plants, spring, summer, and fall, the depth of snows, the strangeness of the skies,—all went down in this note-book. To his memory he never trusted for a fact, but to the page and the pencil, and the abstract in the pocket, not the Journal. I have seen bits of this note-book, but never recognized any word in it; and I have read its expansion in the Journal, in many pages, of that which occupied him but five minutes to write in the field" (*Poet-Naturalist*).

Thoreau's field notes provided the raw material for the creation of a personal mythology: "Facts should only be as the frame to my pictures; they should be material to the mythology which I am writing; not facts to assist men to make money, farmers to farm profitably, in any common sense; facts to tell who I am, and where I have been or what I have thought." Perhaps this offered the ultimate form of self-fulfillment, especially for a literary artist like Thoreau—to create a personal mythology. To fashion a carefully cultivated view of the self from the raw material of his sauntering experiences was Thoreau's greatest writing challenge. In much the same way that Ben Franklin helped create a personal mythology by depicting himself in his "Autobiography" as a young man walking into Philadelphia—an industrious but inexperienced capitalist and an ideal representative of the Puritan work ethic, Thoreau converted the facts of his walking experience into the public self that emerges in his published writings.

In order to accumulate the facts that would make possible his written mythology, Thoreau recorded his observations and sensations during each walk. As with any other aspect of his walking experience, he allowed nothing to interfere with his goals. He even took notes during night walks, despite the poor lighting. Regarding one evening's ramble, he recorded, "I was compelled to stand to write where a soft, faint light from the western sky came in between two willows." Another evening, he was attracted during his walk to some burning stumps in a field, and he used the light from the burning stumps for writing his notes: "I sit on the untouched end of a stump, and warm me by it, and write by the light, the moon not having risen." During this note-taking experience, Thoreau found that the environment affected his note taking as much as it did the walking experience itself: "The moon comes out of the mackeral cloud, and the traveller rejoices. How can man write the same thoughts by the light of the moon, resting his book on a rail by the side of a remote potato-field, that he does by the light of the sun, on his study table? The light is but a luminousness. My pencil seems to move through a creamy, mystic medium." Thoreau took advantage of any available light and special environmental conditions to record his field notes.

Thoreau's field notes offered him the advantage of spontaneity; colored by the immediate walking environment, they helped establish the tone for his later writings. These notes formed the nucleus for his serious writing, which was drawn from his walking experience, and which occurred after varying periods of reflection. In time the Alpha state revelations were transformed into meaningful prose, but a certain incubation stage was required to make this possible. In his *Journal* he notes: "Our ecstatic states, which appear to yield so little fruit, have this value at least: though in the seasons when our genius reigns we may be powerless for expression, yet, in calmer seasons, when our talent is active, the memory of those rarer moods comes to color our picture and is the permanent paint-pot, as it were, into which we dip our brush. . . . They lend the writer when the moment comes a certain superfluity of wealth, making his expression to overrun and float itself."

Waiting a while before doing serious writing helped Thoreau, as it has many other authors, write a more effective account of his walking experience: "I find some advantage in describing the experience of a day on the day following. At this distance it is more ideal, like the landscape seen with the head inverted, or reflections in water."

Because of the effect of his field notes on his later writings, Thoreau's works ring with the testimony of personal experience: "The forcible writer stands bodily behind his words with his experience. He does not make books out of books, but he has been *there* in person." There is always a sense of presence in his writing that draws the reader into the walking experience that is being described. The experience is paramount, the writing secondary—"My life has been the poem I would have writ, / But I could not both live and utter it" (*Poems*)—but the experience takes on new meaning and power because of Thoreau's written expression of it.

Once Thoreau had sauntered, taken his field notes, and allowed time for reflection, he was ready to make his *Journal* entries—the *Journal* being the phase of his writing process in which he first attempted to seriously articulate his walking experiences.

The *Journal* was a significant part of Thoreau's life. He wrote in his *Journal* from the time he was twenty years old until 1861, when poor health prevented those walks which provided material for the *Journal*. The *Journal* represents Thoreau's best effort to shape his walking experiences into a significant personal mythology.

Alfred Kazin credits the strength of Thoreau's prose in

his *Journal* to his walking experience: "Without these excited daily inroads into the fields, Thoreau could never have found the measure for his prose. . . . Thoreau . . . wrote as if a sentence were not even true unless you heard it first ring against the ground."

Thoreau's *Journal* is his major literary work; it contains the fullest account of his life. Nearly all of his other writings are derived and refashioned from it. The fact that Thoreau's walking experience is such a focus of his *Journal* reinforces its importance in his life and demonstrates how inseparable it was from the other aspects of his existence. The numerous *Journal* passages already cited in this study help verify this.

Thoreau, however, did not confine the literary treatment of his walks to his *Journal*. Since most of his non-*Journal* writings were drawn from the *Journal*, it is not surprising that walking plays such a major role in nearly every essay or book that he wrote.

In particular, Thoreau mastered the form known as the excursion, and he published several essays by that title. Literary excursions were very popular in Thoreau's time, but Thoreau's excursions were not written merely to appeal to the popular taste. As an artist he felt the need to write about his walking experiences, to discover the meaning of those experiences through the medium of reflective composition. His excursions are more transcendental and more revelatory about the self than are many of the samples of this genre drawn from his day.

Walking is central in nearly all of them, but what varies from essay to essay is the change in persona that Thoreau utilizes as he presents the experience of each walk in terms unique to himself. In "A Walk to Wachusett" Thoreau poses as a leisured, highly literate philosopher, ever mindful of man's universal experience yet isolated and set apart by position and perspective. The saunterer's generalizations about man's experience provide the focus for much of this excursion piece, as illustrated by these examples: "In the spaces of thought are the reaches of land and water, where men go and come"; "So soon did we, wayfarers, begin to learn that man's life is rounded with the same few facts, the same simple relations everywhere, and it is vain to travel to find it new"; and "There is, however, this consolation to the most wayworn traveler, upon the dustiest road, that the path his feet describe is so perfectly symbolical of human life,—now climbing the hills, now descending into the vale." Several references to Homer and Virgil and the fact that the walker reads Virgil and Wordsworth "with new pleasure" during the excursion sets the highly literary tone that marks this piece. Throughout this essay, the saunterer loiters, reclines, bathes in mountain streams, reflects, and observes. The leisured pace, the literary allusions, and the philosophical observations all contribute to a carefully groomed picture of a reflective, wise walker, widely read and well traveled, who saunters casually through the landscape.

In "A Winter Walk" a different persona emerges. Here Thoreau presents the walker who celebrates the moral purity of nature and saunters with nature as with a friend. He hopes "to borrow some pure and steadfast virtue" from "the cleansed air," and he finds companionship with "the chickadee and nuthatch [which] are more inspiring society than statesmen and philosophers." The saunterer's intimate familiarity with nature is revealed through personification. The woods "are glad and warm still, and as genial and cheery in winter as in summer." A pleasant lake is "nature's saloon, where she has sat down to her toilet. . . . The sun comes with his evaporation to sweep the dust from its surface each morning." He fancies the pond like "the interior of a larger house." Thoreau humanizes nature and feels at one with it.

McIntosh notes that in all of these excursions pieces Thoreau "is a saunterer who must be up to what he sees and tastes, but in each case he is projected somewhat differently: an educated savage-saunterer in 'Walking,' a self-pleased curmudgeon-saunterer in 'Wild Apples,' a poet-saunterer in 'Autumnal Tints,' and a naturalist-saunterer in 'The Succession of Forest Trees.'" The particular picture of the self that is presented in each of these pieces helps distinguish them from one another. Each distinct view of the self contributes to the personal mythology that evolves from all of the published works.

Excursions was published after Thoreau's death, and each of these essays varies, not only in persona, but in theme or emphasis. Walking is central to each piece, but how walking is presented varies according to the perspective that Thoreau wishes to share. For example, in "A Walk to Wachusett" Thoreau compares his ascent of the mountain to the notion that life is like climbing hills and then descending into the valley. In "A Winter Walk" he pictures the cyclical nature of human experience as he describes leaving the town to hike in the countryside and then returning to the town again.

As with these two excursions, walking supplies the structuring principle for several of Thoreau's writings. According to John Broderick, each writing is shaped after the walking pattern in the following manner: "The 'walk' supplies the structural thread for 'Walking,' 'A Walk to Wachusett,' 'A Winter Walk,' and *Cape Cod.* The extended walk or 'journey' serves for *The Maine Woods, A Week on the Concord and Merrimack Rivers,* a 'water walk' with occasional scrambling along the bank. Even 'Civil Disobedience' records what its author calls 'a long journey,' the result of 'traveling into a far country,' and the dislocations of life arraigned in 'Slavery in Massachusetts' symbolically culminate in this: 'The remembrance of my country spoils my walk. . . .' *Walden* itself might be regarded as a year-long walk, for as in his daily walk Thoreau moved away from the mundane world of the village toward one of heightened awareness and potentiality, only to return spiritually reinvigorated, so *Walden* records an adventuring on life which structurally starts from and returns to the world of quiet desperation." Most of Thoreau's writings are patterned after his walking experience.

Walking not only influenced Thoreau's writings thematically, it also affected the organization and style of his prose pieces. For pedestrian authors like Thoreau, sauntering provides the perfect approach to walking in nature and to writing. Sauntering in nature and sauntering on the page are both open-ended and free-flowing experiences. Thoreau's writings are loosely structured; his prose leisurely saunters from page to page as he pursues the emerging meaning of his experience. A good example is Thoreau's essay "Walking." Its rambling, discursive flow of thought appropriately parallels the nature of the sauntering experience and frees the writer to follow the course of his thinking in the way that his feet and mind follow the magnetic pull of nature during a walk. The destination in both cases is ill defined, but the experience is effectively recorded.

One mark of Thoreau's writing style is the way that he creates an appropriate sense of atmosphere for the subject he is writing about; his descriptions seem drawn directly from the particular walking situation, as indeed they were in field-note form.

So well matched were his descriptions to his subjects, that Thoreau lost little if anything when switching from the experience in the field to a written account of it. His sensitivity to this is apparent in the following *Journal* entry, which presents his concern about a writing style appropriate for depicting night walking experiences: "I have not put darkness, duskiness, enough into my night and moonlight walks. Every sentence should contain some twilight or night. At least the light in it should be the yellow or creamy light of the moon or the fine beams of stars, and not the white light of day. The peculiar dusky serenity of the sentences must not allow the reader to forget that it is evening or night, without my saying that it is dark. Otherwise he will, of course, presume a daylight atmosphere.''

Thoreau held the same concern that his writing naturally reflect the sauntering environment in his longer works, including his *A Week on the Concord and Merrimack Rivers:* "I thought that one peculiarity of my 'Week' was its hypaethral character, to use an epithet applied to those Egyptian temples which are open to the heavens above, *under the ether.* I thought that it had little of the atmosphere of the house about it, but might wholly have been written; as in fact it was to a considerable extent, out-of-doors.''

Thoreau's walks affected his prose style in several ways. The active nature of his rambles, and the many adventures that he encountered while sauntering, infused his prose with a sense of exuberance and vitality that he saw lacking in the writing of others whose compositions were not drawn from the deep well of personal experience: "A writer who does not speak out of a full experience uses torpid words, wooden or lifeless words, such words as 'humanity,' which have a paralysis in their tails.'' The rhythmical pattern of walking can be discerned in Thoreau's sentences; many sentences seem like individual steps taken by the saunterer. The rhythm of the walk, and the close contact of the walker's feet with the landscape, find expression in the cadences and concrete description that characterize so much of Thoreau's prose.

One aspect of Thoreau's writing, which reveals the important role that sauntering played in his life, is his use of walking as a metaphor in his works. Walking provided Thoreau with an appropriate symbol for many of his most trenchant observations about life. He felt that one's life should be experienced like an extended walk or journey: "Our life should be so active and progressive as to be a journey." Walking provided him with the appropriate symbol to describe the pathway of life that all must travel: "There is, however, this consolation to the most way-worn traveler, upon the dustiest road, that the path his feet describe is so perfectly symbolical of human life,— now climbing the hills, now descending into the vales."

In particular, Thoreau liked to use walking as a meta-phor for the rigors of life. In *A Week* he writes: "I am astonished at the singular pertinacity and endurance of our lives. The miracle is, that what is *is*, when it is so difficult, if not impossible, for any thing else to be; that we walk on in our particular paths so far, before we fall on death and fate, merely because we must walk some path. . . . We wonder superfluously when we hear of a somnambulist walking a plank securely,—we have walked a plank all our lives up to this particular string-piece where we are.

One's progress in life, impeded and hindered by life's difficulties and surprises, parallels the course of the walker who, according to Thoreau's *Journal*, "advances in his walk somewhat as a river does, meanderingly." In a letter to H. G. O. Blake, Thoreau insists that one's goal in life should be like that of the walker—to proceed on the right path and to try and avoid the undesirable byways and detours that life can send one's way: "If one hesi-tates in his path, let him not proceed. Let him respect his doubts, for doubts, too, may have some divinity in them. . . . When, in the progress of life, a man swerves, though only by an angle infinitely small, from his proper and allotted path . . . , then the drama of his life turns to tragedy, and makes haste to its fifth act."

188

Walking also served Thoreau as a metaphor for representing the pitfalls of conformity. In his *Journal* he comments: "We go about these days as if we had fetters on our feet. We walk in the stocks, stepping into the holes made by our predecessors." A more familiar passage in *Walden* expresses this same concept in more poetic terms: "The surface of the earth is soft and impressible by the feet of men; and so with the paths which the mind travels. How worn and dusty, then, must be the highways of the world, how deep the ruts of tradition and conformity!" Walking, for Thoreau, was a very personal and individual action. Even as he pursued his own course during his walks, unmindful of the paths others took, so one should walk through life as an individualist: "I delight to come to my bearings,—not walk in procession with pomp and parade, in a conspicuous place, but to walk even with the Builder of the universe, if I may,—not live in this restless, nervous, bustling, trivial Nineteenth Century, but stand or sit thoughtfully while it goes by" (*Walden*).

Thoreau was particularly struck by what he perceived as the isolation of life that paralleled his own solitary walking experience. In his *Journal* he reflects: "How alone must our life be lived— We dwell on the sea-shore and none between us and the sea— Men are my merry companions—my fellow pilgrims—who beguile the way, but leave me at the first turn in the road—for none are travelling *one* road so far as myself."

Another aspect of the walking experience that Thoreau metaphorically applied to life is the way that things happen unexpectedly or subconsciously to the walker, and to the person living his life: "There is always some accident in the best things, whether thoughts or expressions or deeds. The memorable thought, the happy expression, the admirable deed are only partly ours. The thought came to us because we were in a fit mood; also we were unconscious and did not know that we had said or done a good thing. We must walk consciously only part way toward our goal, and then leap in the dark to our success."

Although Thoreau used "walking" metaphorically to convey a number of ideas, this term generally carries a positive connotation in his writing. In his *Journal*, sauntering is the activity that he associates with human progress—"Our experience does not wear upon us. It is seen to be fabulous or symbolical, and the future is worth expecting. Encouraged, I set out once more to climb the mountain of the earth, for my steps are symbolical steps, and in all my walking I have not reached the top of the earth yet"; and it is the activity that most accurately represents the history of a human life—"A traveller! I love his title. A traveller is to be reverenced as such. His profession is the best symbol of our life. Going from _____toward_____; it is the history of every one of us." Thoreau envisioned life according to the terms of his own experiences, and certainly his use of "walking" as a metaphor in his writing helps us not only better understand his ideas, but also to better understand that the history of his own life was essentially a walk from one place to another, a journey inward toward the essential self.

6

THOREAU TODAY

Thoreau's walking experience offers much to us today. Consider the picture of man and of human experience that emerges in the various accounts of his walking experience. Although one of Thoreau's major tenets was a belief in simplicity, his saunterings reveal the very complex nature of human personality and human experience. One sees Thoreau the saunterer as a figure who walks into the countryside seeking a delicate balance between the components of his own makeup; in each walk the physical, emotional, mental, and spiritual aspects of his being interact and cooperate as he seeks a fulfilling walking experience. While his feet plant themselves firmly on the ground, his emotions alter according to sensory stimuli, his thoughts flow—triggered by the surrounding environment and his corresponding mood—and his spirit soars, launched by the spiritual truths suggested by the landscape or by intuitions within himself.

While Thoreau saunters externally, carefully observing every surface feature of the landscape, he saunters internally, discovering worlds within as well as worlds without. Thus he relates to different levels of reality at the same time, entertaining the physical world through the aid of his senses, while, simultaneously, plunging into the realm of the mind and the spirit. During this experience, the ever-changing influences of the landscape and the walking conditions, and the state of his own attitude and mood supply a dynamic that determines the final outcome of the walking experience. As a saunterer, then, Thoreau projects the holistic man confronting the realities of the biosphere in which he lives, and his walks readily serve as parables for the very complex interaction between man and his environment, which provides the basis for much of human experience.

Thoreau's walks also reveal as much about the specific nature of his own version of transcendentalism as does any other aspect of his experience. Perhaps no figure better illustrates the transcendental emphasis on the organic nature of human personality and man's relation to the environment than Thoreau does through his walking experience. In fact, all of the basic transcendental beliefs that Thoreau held are demonstrated in his walking experience. His bent toward simplicity, solitude, individualism, economy, and other transcendental notions are revealed as much in his sauntering experience as they are in his experience at Walden Pond.

Thoreau discovered and articulated his transcendental view of life while at Walden, but he applied that view every time he took a walk. One can readily observe in his walking experience the thing that probably set him the most apart from Emerson, Alcott, and other transcendentalists—his determined commitment to apply the principles of transcendentalism to life. Walden was only a two-year experiment in this, but Thoreau's walks involved a daily application of his beliefs to a life that he chose to live on his own terms, forsaking what his contemporaries considered a regular vocation to commit himself to his avocation—sauntering. The conflicts that a transcendentalist experiences when applying an idealistic philosophy to life are frequently illustrated in Thoreau's attempts to dissociate himself from the city influence while somehow maintaining and nurturing his ties to society, and his efforts to respond to the magnetic pull of nature while granting priority to the role of human experience in shaping the significance of his walks. One sees in Thoreau's walking experience all the tensions that exist between the tenets of transcendentalism and the prevailing beliefs in orthodoxy and protestant work ethic held by the majority in his own time.

Thoreau's saunters are significant, as well, for what they reveal about him as a person. Through his rambles, we see his personality—revealed in his walking gait and in the various ways that he applies himself to the different walking tasks. We see his interests, his sense of humor, his several idiosyncrasies, his particularity, his bounding physical energy, his practicality, his dogged tenacity—each aspect of his personality reveals itself through his sauntering adventures. As the central activity of his life, Thoreau's walks reveal more about him as a person than one can glean from studying any other single aspect of his life. They form an integral part of his biography.

And certainly one very important side of Thoreau—his attraction to nature—is better revealed in his walking experience than anywhere else. The paramount role that his senses played in his rambles accounts for the participatory nature of his walking experience, and the resulting intimate relationship with a maternal nature that he enjoyed. For Thoreau each saunter was a sort of primitive rite celebrating the movements and rhythms of nature; and the eating, drinking, bathing, and wading that he engaged in during his walks reveal his deep desire to immerse himself in the landscape, to absorb nature within himself and to become one with the environment. In order to understand Thoreau's complex relationship with nature, one must consider his walking experience, for his walks placed him in nature and governed every aspect of his experience with the landscape.

Perhaps one of the most important aspects of Thoreau's

walking experience is its connection with his writing process and with his published writings. Many of Thoreau's writings originated with the notes he took in the field during his walks, and they present a literary heritage that preserves the personal mythology he so carefully crafted. When reading his works, particularly those that most directly relate to his walks, one sees Thoreau as a man who lives a border life between civilization and the wilderness and who bridges these two worlds with his walks. The personal mythology Thoreau presents reveals a rugged individual, a pioneer figure, who, like Natty Bumpo, maintains his ties to society while experiencing in nature the personal and spiritual renewal that his self requires. Thoreau's literary persona allies itself with figures like Natty and Huckleberry Finn, who portray the qualities of the frontiersman and the romantic adventurer. This perspective emerges from the walks he took, which spanned the border world he lived in and provided the adventure and experiences that fulfilled him and gave his life meaning.

Certainly the paramount role of walking in Thoreau's writings evidences the significant role of his walking experience; studying his walking experience helps one better understand Thoreau's craft as a writer, his special ability to fashion experience into art. Walking provides a thematic key to the *Journal*, his most ambitious literary work. As a result, walking surfaces as a theme or major factor in most of Thoreau's other writings that find their source in the *Journal*. And even his prose style and organization often reflect the nature of his walking experience in some of his writings, such as the excursion piece "Walking."

Thoreau is a significant figure, not simply as a writer, but as a walker as well. In his own time, walking helped connect him with other literary saunterers, the most obvious group being literary naturalists. These men explored nature in order to discover its secrets and to experience its delights. They produced a considerable body of literature, the result of their perambulatory excursions into nature. Their writings, like Thoreau's literary treatment of his own naturalist experience, reveal an important relationship between walking in nature and writing about it. Thoreau was the main writer-naturalist in New England, but in other parts of the country many other literary naturalists fulfilled the same role, including John Muir, Gilbert White, John Burroughs, William Bartram, and John James Audubon.

Thoreau even owed, in part, his relationships with Walt Whitman, Ralph Waldo Emerson, and Nathaniel Hawthorne to his walking experience. Like Thoreau, these men were walkers as well as writers, and their shared walking experience provided them with common ground that made a relationship easier to form and to keep. Certainly this was the case with Whitman and Thoreau. When Thoreau and Alcott first visited Whitman, he informed them that his daily schedule usually involved reading and writing in the morning and walking in the afternoon, the same walking schedule that Thoreau practiced. Thoreau acknowledged the popularity of this schedule among literary walkers when he wrote in a letter that Whitman "now has no employment but to read and write in the forenoon, and walk in the afternoon, like all the rest of the scribbling gentry" (*Correspondence*). Whitman and Thoreau shared several walks together, finding common ground in the walking experience even if their own applications of transcendentalism differed.

Thoreau's walking experience was apparently responsible for his first contact with Ralph Waldo Emerson. George Hoar, a contemporary of Thoreau's, recalls that Emerson was so impressed by the fact that Thoreau had walked eighteen miles to hear one of his lectures that he invited Thoreau to his house to hear a lecture there.

Emerson, like Thoreau, held a very high view of walking. He stated in "Country Life": "I think 'tis the best of humanity that goes out to walk. In happy hours, I think all affairs may be wisely postponed for this walking." In somewhat typical fashion, Emerson could articulate a high ideal, in this case the laudability of walking, but he seldom applied his stated ideals to his own experience. He walked, but not with the fervor or commitment of Thoreau, who happily postponed "all affairs" whenever he could to make walking possible.

Although both men conceived walking in much the same way—Emerson considered walking an art form, much as Thoreau did—their type of walking experience differed significantly. Emerson favored brief walks, Thoreau long, difficult ones. Thoreau's brand of sauntering was considerably more arduous than Emerson's. John Muir's essay, "Emerson at Yosemite," reveals Emerson's aversion to the kind of difficult, lengthy walks that Thoreau thoroughly enjoyed. The concept of walking united Thoreau with several of his contemporaries, including Whitman, Emerson, and Nathaniel Hawthorne, who Thoreau took several walks with, but his application of walking set him apart from each of these men. Probably no man of his time was so completely committed to walking as Thoreau was.

One thing that is quite impressive about Thoreau's walking experience is the influence that it has had since his time. This influence is readily measurable in terms of subsequent walkers duplicating his walks or attempting to practice walking in a particular way that Thoreau defined or exemplified. In his book *Thoreau's Method: A Handbook for Nature Study* David Pepi illustrates the popular interest in Thoreau's walking method. Pepi devotes an entire chapter to a guide to walking based on Thoreau's own walking methodology. In spite of Pepi's enthusiasm for Thoreau, he is not always faithful to Thoreau's walking method. For example, he cautions against taking shortcuts through planted fields, although Thoreau had little reservation about doing this. Still, Pepi's book is representative of efforts writers have made to study and advocate Thoreau's walking methods.

Even more common than walking guides influenced by Thoreau are the many published accounts of walkers' attempts to replicate actual walking trips that Thoreau took. Typical is Caroline Bates's article, "Walking in Thoreau's Footsteps on Cape Cod," in which she recounts one of Thoreau's own Cape Cod trips and depicts the conditions of the Cape today, which a walker, following Thoreau's original course, would face. A similar article by Joseph Thorndike, "Thoreau Walks the Cape," does much the same. One pedestrian writer describes what a trip to Maine in 1948 had to offer similar to Thoreau's own trip to the same area years before. Characteristic is this sample observation: "In the ninety-one years since Thoreau made the trip, the millions of acres of scattered lakes in the northwest corner of the state have changed less than most parts of America. Unbroken by roads and towns, with perhaps less than a dozen permanent residents, the woods are today as they were . . . one hundred years ago. There is no need to grope for the past. It exists before your eyes as part of the unchanging present of the mountains, lakes and streams that Thoreau crossed and remembered" (Wylie, "Thoreau Trails").

Walkers like Wylie and the naturalist Edwin Way Teale seem to pride themselves on their ability to duplicate a Thoreau walk under modern conditions. Teale's boastful account of Concord sauntering seems especially well suited to a Thoreauvian hiker: "'I can easily walk,' Thoreau wrote in his *Journal*, 'ten, fifteen, twenty, any number of miles, commencing at my own door, without going by any house, without crossing a road except where the fox and the mink do.' But, in the main, so little changed is

197

Walden and its surroundings that on my first visit, I found my way around without difficulty by means of a map in the front of one of the volumes of H. G. O. Blake's selections from Thoreau's *Journal*, a map that had been made in the year 1852."

Yet another evidence of Thoreau's influence on American walkers is the way authors writing about walking use Thoreau and his sauntering experience as a reference point. One writer, describing a particular part of the epic hike of Edward Garvey, who walked the 2,205 miles of the Appalachian Trail, makes this reference: "Garvey took his time the rest of the way, maintaining that 'like Thoreau, I felt rich in sunny summer days, and I spent them lavishly'" (Thompson). Another author, Donald Peattie, celebrates that "America, land of the motor car, land of the rubber tire, is going off wheels and learning to walk. Of this I sing." In his article, "The Joy of Walking," Peattie shares the personal rewards he derives from walking. Philosophizing, he claims that the time spent walking is well invested. "For after all, time is not money; time is an opportunity to live before you die. So a man who walks, and lives and sees and thinks as he walks, has lengthened his life." He follows with this appropriate reference to Thoreau: "It was Thoreau, himself one of the most inveterate of walkers, who insisted that if you took the train from Concord to Fitchburg, and he took shanks' mare, he would arrive first. For, he reasoned, you would have to stop and work till you had earned the price of a ticket. While you were doing that he would be in Scotland afore ye. And have seen enough sights and had enough encounters to write another immortal chapter."

A similar reference to Thoreau as a walker appears in an article, "The Walker." The anonymous author describes "a stroller who gets his pleasure from what he hears and sees on his stroll," and then speculates: "Yet isn't this stroller with his dilettante legs a distant relation of the saunterer, the perfect and rare walker, only one or two specimens of which Thoreau had ever seen? Of the true transcendental walker, the crusader Henry was perhaps the sole example." As with these previous examples, those Americans dedicated to walking find it natural to refer to Thoreau and his experience. John Davis, no exception to this, begins a point by referring to Thoreau's view that "walking is priceless." He concludes that "this is even more true now than in Thoreau's day," and he proceeds to advocate the type of nonmaterialistic recreation that Thoreau-style walking provides.

One way Thoreau has influenced American walkers is by inspiring future generations to participate in the sauntering experience. Ann Zwinger, in a delightful article, "The Quintessential Wanderer," defines this aspect of Thoreau's contribution: "Wandering is a solitary practice, yet those of us who are wanderers can never walk alone. We walk with those who have gone before, and found their sanity where we find ours: in the dew-frosted thistle or the dragonfly's patrol, in the coiled fern frond, or the summer rose." She adds that Thoreau's walking experience "reaches out to entice us to wander. He could have given us no greater gift."

Thoreau's walking experience has set a standard by which subsequent saunterers have measured their walking experience. John Finley, a prolific and prominent American walker, designed a medal to give to walkers that bore the inscription "'a la Sainte Terre,'—to the Holy Land." He writes, "I am indebted for this legend to Thoreau," and goes on to describe the quality of the walking experience that Thoreau exemplified and that his medal commemorates: "A real pilgrim is no idler or vagabond or aimless vagrant; he is a destinated person, a walker, a 'hiker,' a wanderer or even a 'saunterer' with a goal, but with an ever-changing prospect." Finley, after quoting Thoreau that "each man's Holy Land lies in so different a direction that it is difficult to say whither his path will lead,'' adds: ''When I award the 'a la Sainte Terre' medal I translate the legend freely as meaning 'to our better selves'—the 'better' meaning both physical and spiritual health, which is reached by most people most certainly by keeping their feet on what that beloved philosopher of the out of doors, Liberty Bailey, has called 'the holy earth.'''

Just as Thoreau's walking experience continues to influence those who commit themselves to the sauntering life today, so it also challenges Thoreauvians to examine it as carefully as they can in order to better understand Thoreau's own life, his beliefs, and his writings. In their own ways Thoreau scholars must follow Alcott's advice and take a walk with Thoreau. Only then can they understand why it was that he could not ''preserve [his] health and spirits'' unless he walked for four or more hours every day, ''sauntering through the woods and over the hills and fields, absolutely free from all worldly engagements.'' Only then can they appreciate how walking was, for Thoreau, ''the enterprise and adventure of the day.''

BIBLIOGRAPHY

Alcott, Amos Bronson. "The Forester." *Atlantic Monthly* 9 (April 1862): 443–445.

———. "Journals." *Thoreau: Man of Concord.* Ed. Walter Harding. New York: Holt, Rinehart and Winston, 1960. 160–165.

———. "Thoreau." *Thoreau: A Century of Criticism.* Ed. Walter Harding. Dallas: Southern Methodist University Press, 1954. 54–58.

Bates, Caroline. "Walking in Thoreau's Footsteps on Cape Cod." *The Gentle Art of Walking.* Ed. George D. Trent. New York: Random House, 1971. 142–143.

Benton, Joel. "Persons and Places." *Thoreau: Man of Concord.* Ed. Walter Harding. New York: Holt, Rinehart and Winston, 1960. 113.

Boller, Paul F., Jr. *American Transcendentalism, 1830–1860, an Intellectual Inquiry.* New York: G. P. Putnam's Sons, 1974.

Borland, Hal. Introduction. *The Gentle Art of Walking.* Ed. George D. Trent. New York: Random House, 1971. v–x.

———. "To Own the Streets and Fields." *The Gentle Art of Walking.* Ed. George D. Trent. New York: Random House, 1971. 11, 12.

Broderick, John C. "The Movement of Thoreau's Prose." *American Literature* 33.2 (1961): 133–142.

Brown, Mary Hosmer. "Memories of Concord." *Thoreau: Man of Concord.* Ed. Walter Harding. New York: Holt, Rinehart and Winston, 1960. 149–152.

Burgess, Edward S. "Notes on Concord People." *Thoreau: Man of Concord*. Ed. Walter Harding. New York: Holt, Rinehart and Winston, 1960. 188, 189.

Burroughs, John. "The Exhilarations of the Road." *The Footpath Way: An Anthology for Walkers*. Ed. Hilaire Belloc. London: Sidgwick & Jackson, Ltd., 1911. 221–240.

———. *The Heart of Burrough's Journals*. Ed. Clara Barrus. Boston: Houghton Mifflin Company, 1928.

———. "Henry D. Thoreau." *Indoor Studies*. Boston: Houghton Mifflin Company, 1904. 3–47. Vol. 8 of *The Writings of John Burroughs*. 15 vols.

Canby, Henry Seidel. *Thoreau*. Boston: Houghton Mifflin Company, 1939.

Carpenter, Frederick Ives. "Transcendentalism." *American Transcendentalism: An Anthology of Criticism*. Ed. Brian M. Barbour. South Bend: University of Notre Dame Press, 1973. 23–34.

Channing, William Ellery. *Thoreau the Poet-Naturalist*. Ed. F. B. Sanborn. 1902. New York: Biblo and Tanner, 1966.

Christie, John Aldrich. *Thoreau as World Traveler*. New York: Columbia University Press, 1965.

Conway, Moncure D. "Thoreau." *Thoreau: Man of Concord*. Ed. Walter Harding. New York: Holt, Rinehart and Winston, 1960. 38–40.

Cook, Reginald L. *Passage to Walden*. 2nd ed. New York: Russell & Russell, 1966.

Couser, G. Thomas. "Thoreau's Cape Cod Pilgrimage." *American Transcendental Quarterly* 26 Supplement (Spring 1975): 31–36.

Crane, Stephen. "A Man Said to the Universe." *The American Tradition in Literature*. Ed. George Perkins et al. 7th ed. Shorter ed. New York: McGraw-Hill, 1900. 1206.

Dabbs, James McBride. "Thoreau: The Adventurer as Economist." *Yale Review* 36 (Summer, 1947): 667–672.

Davis, John T. *Walking!* Kansas City: Andrews and McMeel, Inc., 1979.

Dillard, Annie. *Pilgrim at Tinker Creek.* New York: Harper & Row, 1974.

Eifert, Virginia S. "The Botanist, Thoreau." *Tall Trees and Far Horizons: Adventures and Discoveries of Early Botanists in America.* New York: Dodd, Mead & Company, 1965. 239–256.

Emerson, Edward Waldo. *Henry Thoreau as Remembered by a Young Friend.* 1917. Concord: Thoreau Foundation, Inc., 1968.

Emerson, Ralph Waldo. *The Complete Works of Ralph Waldo Emerson.* Centenary Edition. 12 vols. New York: AMS Press, 1979.

———. *The Journals and Miscellaneous Notebooks of Ralph Waldo Emerson.* Ralph H. Orth, et al., eds. 16 vols. Cambridge, Mass.: Harvard University Press, 1960–1982.

———. "Thoreau." *Thoreau: A Century of Criticism.* Ed. Walter Harding. Dallas: Southern Methodist University Press, 1954. 22–40.

Finley, John H. "Long Highway Beckons to the Walker." *The Gentle Art of Walking.* Ed. George D. Trent. New York: Random House, 1971. 4, 5.

Fussell, Edwin S. "The Red Face of Man." *Thoreau: A Collection of Critical Essays.* Ed. Sherman Paul. Englewood Cliffs, N.J.: Prentice Hall, Inc., 1962.

Gale, Bill. *The Wonderful World of Walking.* New York: William Morrow and Company, Inc., 1979.

Garber, Frederick. *Thoreau's Redemptive Imagination.* New York: New York University Press, 1977.

Harding, Walter. *The Days of Henry Thoreau.* New York: Alfred A. Knopf, 1970.

————, and Michael Meyer. *The New Thoreau Handbook.* New York: New York University Press, 1980.

Heidegger, Martin. "What Is Metaphysics." *Basic Writings.* Ed. David Krell. New York: Harper & Row, 1977. 91–112.

Higginson, Samuel Storrow. "Henry D. Thoreau." *Thoreau: Man of Concord.* Ed. Walter Harding. New York: Holt, Rinehart and Winston, 1960. 10–14.

Hoar, George F. "Autobiography of Seventy Years." *Thoreau: Man of Concord.* Ed. Walter Harding. New York: Holt, Rinehart and Winston, 1960. 109, 110.

Huth, Hans. *Nature and the American: Three Centuries of Changing Attitudes.* Berkeley: University of California Press, 1957.

Jenison, Madge. "About Roads." *The Magic of Walking.* Ed. Aaron Sussman and Ruth Goode. New York: Simon and Schuster, 1967. 378–384.

Jenkins, Peter. *A Walk Across America.* New York: Morrow, 1979.

————, and Barbara Jenkins. *The Walk West: A Walk Across America, and Across China.* New York: Fawcett, 1981.

Kazin, Alfred. "Thoreau's Journals." *Thoreau: A Century of Criticism.* Ed. Walter Harding. Dallas: Southern Methodist University, 1954. 187–191.

Krock, Arthur. "Earlier Links Between Presidents and Hiking." *The Gentle Art of Walking.* Ed. George D. Trent. New York: Randon House, 1971. 35, 36.

Krutch, Joseph Wood. *Henry David Thoreau.* New York: William Sloane Associates, 1948.

Lane, Lauriat, Jr. "Thoreau's Two Walks: Structure and Meaning." *The Thoreau Society Bulletin* 109 (Fall 1969): 1–4.

Lebeaux, Richard. *Young Man Thoreau.* Amherst: University of Massachusetts Press, 1977.

Lowell, James Russell. "Thoreau." *Thoreau: A Century of Criticism.* Ed. Walter Harding. Dallas: Southern Methodist University Press, 1954. 44–53.

Matthiessen, F. O. *American Renaissance: Art and Expression in the Age of Emerson and Whitman.* New York: Oxford University Press, 1941.

McIntosh, James. *Thoreau as Romantic Naturalist: His Shifting Stance Toward Nature.* Ithaca, New York: Cornell University Press, 1974.

Muir, John. "Emerson at Yosemite." *The Magic of Walking.* Ed. Aaron Sussman and Ruth Goode. New York: Simon and Schuster, 1967. 273–276.

Paul, Sherman. *The Shores of America: Thoreau's Inward Exploration.* Urbana, Illinois: The University of Illinois Press, 1958.

Peattie, Donald Culross. "The Joy of Walking." *The Gentle Art of Walking.* Ed. George D. Trent. New York: Random House, 1971. 7, 8.

Pepi, David. *Thoreau's Method: A Handbook for Nature Study.* Englewood Cliffs, New Jersey: Prentice-Hall, Inc., 1985.

Richardson, Robert D., Jr. *Henry Thoreau: A Life of the Mind.* Berkeley: University of California Press, 1986.

Sanborn, F. B. "The Personality of Thoreau." *Thoreau: Man of Concord.* Ed. Walter Harding. New York: Holt, Rinehart and Winston, 1960. 98.

Schneider, Richard J. *Henry David Thoreau.* Boston: Twayne Publishers, 1987.

Stearns, Frank Preston. "Sketches from Concord and Appledore." *Thoreau: Man of Concord.* Ed. Walter Harding. New York: Holt, Rinehart and Winston, 1960. 78, 79.

Stevenson, Robert Louis. "Henry David Thoreau: His Character and Opinions." *Thoreau: A Century of Criticism.* Ed. Walter Harding. Dallas: Southern Methodist University Press, 1954. 59–83.

Stowell, Robert F. *A Thoreau Gazetteer*. Ed. William L. Howarth. Princeton, New Jersey: Princeton University Press, 1970.

Sussman, Aaron, and Ruth Goode, eds. *The Magic of Walking*. New York: Simon and Schuster, 1967.

Teale, Edwin Way. *The Lost Woods: Adventures of a Naturalist*. New York: Dodd, Mead & Company, 1945.

Thomas, Stephen W. "Notes of a Conversation." *Thoreau: Man of Concord*. Ed. Walter Harding. New York: Holt, Rinehart and Winston, 1960. 192.

Thomson, Peggy. "55 Men, Women and Grandfathers Have Hiked All 2,025 Miles of the Appalachian Trail." *The Gentle Art of Walking*. Ed. George D. Trent. New York: Random House, 1971. 94–99.

Thoreau, Henry David. *Collected Poems of Henry Thoreau*. Ed. Carl Bode. Enl. ed. Baltimore: The Johns Hopkins Press, 1964.

———. *The Correspondence of Henry Thoreau*. Ed. Walter Harding and Carl Bode. New York: New York University Press, 1958.

———. *Early Essays and Miscellanies*. Ed. Joseph J. Moldenhauer, Edwin Moser, and Alexander C. Kern. Princeton, New Jersey: Princeton University Press, 1975.

———. *Huckleberries*. Ed. Leo Stoller. Preface Alexander C. Kern. New York: The New York City Public Library, 1970.

———. *The Journal of Henry D. Thoreau*. Ed. Bradford Torrey and Frances H. Allen. 1906. Foreword by Walter Harding. New York: Dover Publications, Inc., 1962. 14 vols. (Bound as 2).

———. *Journal Vol. 1: 1837–1844*. Ed. Elizabeth Hale Witherell, et al. Princeton, New Jersey: Princeton University Press, 1981.

———. *Journal Vol. 2: 1842–1848*. Ed. Robert Sattelmeyer.

Princeton, New Jersey: Princeton University Press, 1984.

———. *The Maine Woods.* Ed. Joseph J. Moldenhauer. Princeton, New Jersey: Princeton University Press, 1972.

———. *Reform Papers.* Ed. Wendell Glick. Princeton, New Jersey: Princeton University Press, 1973.

———. *Walden.* Ed. J. Lyndon Shanley. Princeton, New Jersey: Princeton University Press, 1971.

———. *A Week on the Concord and Merrimack Rivers.* Ed. Carl F. Hovde, William L. Howarth, and Elizabeth Witherell. Princeton, New Jersey: Princeton University Press, 1980.

———. *The Writings of Henry David Thoreau.* Walden Edition. Boston: The Riverside Press, 1906. 20 vols.

Thorndike, Joseph J., Jr. "Thoreau Walks the Cape." *American Heritage* 38.3 (April 1987): 71–75.

Traubel, Horace. "With Walt Whitman in Camden." *Thoreau: Man of Concord.* Ed. Walter Harding. New York: Holt, Rinehart and Winston, 1960. 116.

Trevelyan, George Macaulay. *Walking.* Hartford, Connecticut: Edwin Valentine Mitchell, 1928.

Vickery, Jim Dale. "The Walking Life: A Thoughtful Stroll with Henry David Thoreau." *Writer's Digest* 61 (September 1981): 64.

"The Walker." *The Gentle Art of Walking.* Ed. George D. Trent. New York: Random House, 1971. 19.

Weiss, John. "Thoreau." *Thoreau: Man of Concord.* Ed. Walter Harding. New York: Holt, Rinehart and Winston, 1960. 32–37.

Whitcomb, Robert. "The Thoreau 'Country.'" *Thoreau: Man of Concord.* Ed. Walter Harding. New York: Holt, Rinehart and Winston, 1960. 154.

Williams, Paul O. "Emerson Guided: Walks with Thoreau

and Channing." *Emerson Society Quarterly* 35.3 (II Quarter 1964): 66–68.

Willson, Lawrence. "Another View of the Pilgrims." *The New England Quarterly* 34.2 (June 1961): 160–177.

Wood, James B. "Thoreau and the Pines." *Thoreau: Man of Concord.* Ed. Walter Harding. New York: Holt, Rinehart and Winston, 1960. 106, 107.

Woodbury, Charles J. "Talks with Ralph Waldo Emerson." *Thoreau: Man of Concord.* Ed. Walter Harding. New York: Holt, Rinehart and Winston, 1960. 65–71.

Worster, Donald. *Nature's Economy: A History of Ecological Ideas.* Cambridge: Cambridge University Press, 1977.

Wright, Richardson. *Hawkers and Walkers in Early America.* Philadelphia: J. B. Lippincott Company, 1927.

Wylie, Evan M. "Thoreau Trails." *Holiday* 4 (Sept. 1948): 105–109, 136.

Zwinger, Ann. "The Quintessential Wanderer." *The Thoreau Society Bulletin* 169 (Fall 1984): 1, 2.

INDEX